D0211061

THE BLUE AND THE GRAY

THE BLUE AND THE GRAY

The Best Poems of the Civil War

Compiled and Edited by

CLAUDIUS MEADE CAPPS

Granger Index Reprint Series

BOOKS FOR LIBRARIES PRESS
FREEPORT, NEW YORK

LIBRARY OF CONGRESS CATALOG CARD NUMBER:
70-75710

FOREWORD

Eighty-two years ago the first shot of the Civil War was fired at Fort Sumter, South Carolina, and seventy-eight years ago peace was declared at Appomattox in Virginia, and signed by General U. S. Grant and General Robert E. Lee, thus closing the Cvil War after four years of struggle. During these four years many poems and song poems were written in both the North and the South. Many of these poems were published in local papers and many of them were not published at all.

With the view of compiling these poems into one book I am publishing this Anthology of the Best Poems of the Civil War. In this undertaking I have been assisted by many of the State Librarians of the different states with the result that I have poems assembled from New Hampshire to Texas, and from Michigan to Florida, covering a cross section of our common country both north and south.

In this effort I want to express my appreciation to these librarians who have rendered valuable assistance in sending me poems, and also made suggestions of poems that they would like included in the Anthology. Three things we have kept in view; first, to select poems of greatest historical value, depicting the leading battles of the war; next, to select poems of pathos that express the deep heart feelings of those who were bereft; and last but not least, to select poems of the best literary value.

Besides the appreciation expressed above I also wish to acknowledge the benefit received from the following books and authors, and to thank Mr. H. U. Felleman of the *New York Times* for furnishing poems that I was unable to locate in any publication: *South in History and Literature*, by Mildred Lewis Rutherford; *American War Songs*, By National Society of Colonial Dames of America; *Best Things From Best Authors*, By J. W. Shoemaker; *Poems of American History*, Edited by Burton Egbert Stevenson; *Heart Songs*, Published by The Chapple Publishing Company of Boston; *Poems and Rhymes*, By Eva March Tappan; *Library of Poetry and Song*, By William Cullen Bryant; *War Songs and Poems of the Southern Confederacy*, By H. M. Wharton, D.D.

THE SOLITARY REAPER

Will no one tell me what she sings?
Perhaps the plaintive numbers flow
For old, unhappy, far-off things,
And battles long ago.

THE BLUE AND THE GRAY

(1867)

By the flow of the inland river,
  Whence the fleets of iron have fled,
Where the blades of the grave-grass quiver,
  Asleep are the ranks of the dead:
    Under the sod and the dew,
      Waiting the judgment-day;
    Under the one, the Blue,
      Under the other, the Gray.

These in the robings of glory,
  Those in the gloom of defeat,
All with the battle-blood gory,
  In the dusk of eternity meet:
    Under the sod and the dew,
      Waiting the judgment-day;
    Under the laurel, the Blue,
      Under the willow, the Gray.

From the silence of sorrowful hours
  The desolate mourners go,
Lovingly laden with flowers
  Alike for the friend and the foe:
    Under the sod and the dew,
      Waiting the judgment-day;
    Under the roses, the Blue,
      Under the lilies, the Gray.

So with an equal splendor,
  The morning sunrays fall,
With a touch impartially tender,
  On the blossoms blooming for all:

Under the sod and the dew,
Waiting the judgment-day;
Broidered with gold, the Blue,
Mellowed with gold, the Gray.

So, when the summer calleth,
On forest and field of grain,
With an equal murmur falleth
The cooling drip of the rain:
Under the sod and the dew,
Waiting the judgment-day;
Wet with the rain, the Blue,
Wet with the rain, the Gray.

Sadly, but not with upbraiding,
The generous deed was done,
In the storm of the years that are fading
No braver battle was won:
Under the sod and the dew,
Waiting the judgment-day;
Under the blossoms, the Blue,
Under the garlands, the Gray.

No more shall the war-cry sever,
Or the winding rivers be red;
They banish our anger forever
When they laurel the graves of our dead!
Under the sod and the dew,
Waiting the judgment-day;
Love and tears for the Blue,
Tears and love for the Gray.

FRANCIS MILES FINCH
(*Mississippi*)

THE CONQUERED BANNER

Furl that Banner, for 'tis weary;
Round its staff 'tis drooping dreary;
  Furl it, fold it, it is best;
For there's not a man to wave it,
And there's not a sword to save it,
And there's not one left to lave it
In the blood which heroes gave it:
And its foes now scorn and brave it;
  Furl it, hide it—let it rest!

Take that banner down! 'tis tattered;
Broken is its staff and shattered;
And the valiant hosts are scattered
  Over whom it floated high.
Oh! 'tis hard for us to fold it;
Hard to think there's none to hold it;
Hard that those who once unrolled it
  Now must furl it with a sigh.

Furl that Banner! furl it sadly!
Once ten thousands hailed it gladly,
And ten thousands wildly, madly,
  Swore it should forever wave;
Swore that foeman's sword should never
Hearts like theirs entwined dissever,
Till that flag should float forever
  O'er their freedom or their grave!

Furl it; for the hands that grasped it,
And the hearts that fondly clasped it,
  Cold and dead are lying low;
And that Banner—it is trailing!
While around it sounds the wailing
  Of its people in their woe.

For, though conquered, they adore it!
Love the cold, dead hands that bore it!
Weep for those who fell before it!
Pardon those who trailed and tore it!
  But, oh! wildly they deplore it,
  Now who furl and fold it so.

Furl that Banner! True, 'tis gory,
Yet 'tis wreathed around with glory,
And 'twill live in song and story,
  Though its folds are in the dust:
For its fame on brightest pages,
Penned by poets and by sages,
Shall go sounding down the ages—
  Furl its folds though now we must.

Furl that Banner, softly, slowly!
Treat it gently—it is holy—
  For it droops above the dead.
Touch it not—unfold it never,
Let it droop there, furled forever,
  For its people's hopes are dead!

ABRAM JOSEPH (FATHER) RYAN
(*Virginia*)

IN STATE

O keeper of the Sacred Key,
And the Great Seal of Destiny,
Whose eye is the blue canopy,
Look down upon the warring world, and tell us what the end will be.

"Lo, through the wintry atmosphere,
On the white bosom of the sphere,
A cluster of five lakes appear;
And all the land looks like a couch, or warrior's shield, or sheeted bier,

"And on that vast and hollow field,
With both lips closed and both eyes sealed,
A mighty Figure is revealed,—
Stretched at full length, and stiff and stark, as in the hollow of a shield.

"The winds have tied the drifted snow
Around the face and chin; and lo,
The sceptred Giants come and go,
And shake their shadowy crowns and say: 'We always feared it would be so!'

"She came of an heroic race:
A giant's strength, a maiden's grace,
Like two in one seem to embrace,
And match, and blend, and thorough-blend, in her colossal form and face.

"Where can her dazzling falchion be!
One hand is fallen in the sea;
The Gulf Stream drifts it far and free;
And in that hand her shining brand gleams from the depths resplendently.

"And by the other, in its rest,
The starry banner of the West
Is clasped forever to her breast;
And of her silver helmet, lo, a soring eagle is the crest.

"And on her brow, a softened light,
As of a star concealed from sight
By some thin veil of fleecy white,
Or of the rising moon behind the raining vapors of the night.

"The Sisterhood that was so sweet,
The Starry System sphered complete,
Which the mazed Orient used to greet,
The Four-and-Thirty fallen Stars glimmer and glitter at her feet.

"And over her,—and over all,
For panoply and coronal,
The mighty Immemorial,
And everlasting Canopy and Starry Arch and Shield of all.

"Three cold, bright moons have marched and wheeled;
And the white cerement that revealed
A Figure stretched upon a Shield,
Is turned to verdure; and the Land is now one mighty Battle-field.

"And lo, the children which she bred,
And more than all else cherished,
To make them true in heart and head,
Stand face to face, as mortal foes, with their swords crossed above the dead.

"Each hath a mighty stroke and stride;
One true,—the more that he is tried;
The other dark and evil-eyed;—
And by the hand of one of them, his own dear mother surely died!

"A stealthy step, a gleam of hell,—
It is the simple truth to tell,—
The Son stabbed and the Mother fell:
And so she lies, all mute and pale, and pure and Irreproachable!

"And then the battle-trumpet blew;
And the true brother sprang and drew
His blade to smite the traitor through;
And so they clashed above the bier, and the Night sweated bloody dew.

"And all their children, far and wide,
That are so greatly multiplied,
Rise up in frenzy and divide;
And choosing, each whom he will serve, unsheathe the sword and take their side.

"And in the low sun's bloodshot rays,
Portentous of the coming days,
The Two great Oceans blush and blaze,
With the emergent continent between them, wrapt in crimson haze.

Now whichsoever stand or fall,
As God is great, and man is small,
The Truth shall triumph over all;
Forever and forevermore, the Truth shall triumph over all!

"I see the champion sword-strokes flash;
I see them fall and hear them clash;
I hear the murderous engines crash;
I see a brother stoop to loose a foeman-brother's bloody sash.

"I see the torn and mangled corse,
The dead and dying heaped in scores,
The headless rider by his horse,
The wounded captive bayoneted through and through without remorse.

"I hear the dying sufferer cry,
With his crushed face turned to the sky,
I see him crawl in agony
To the foul pool, and bow his head into bloody slime, and die.

"I see the assassin crouch and fire,
I see his victim fall,—expire;
I see the murderer creeping nigher
To strip the dead. He turns the head,—the face! The son beholds his sire!

"I hear the curses and the thanks;
I see the mad charge on the flanks,
The rents, the gaps, the broken ranks,
The vanquished squadrons driven headlong down the river's bridgeless banks.

"I see the death-gripe on the plain,
The grappling monsters on the main,
The tens of thousands that are slain,
And all the speechless suffering and agony of heart and brain.

"I see the dark and bloody spots,
The crowded rooms and crowded cots,
The bleaching bones, the battle blots,—
And writ on many a nameless grave, a legend of forget-me-nots.

"I see the gorged prison-den,
The dead line and the pent-up pen,
The thousands quartered in the fen,
The living-deaths of skin and bone that were the goodly shapes of men.

"And still the bloody Dew must fall!
And His great Darkness with the Pall
Of His dread Judgment cover all,
Till the Dead Nation rise Transformed by Truth to triumph over all!

"And Last—and Last I see—The Deed."
Thus saith the Keeper of the Key,
And the Great Seal of Destiny,
Whose eye is the blue canopy,
And leaves the Pall of His great Darkness over all the Land and Sea.

FORCEYTHE WILLSON
(*Indiana*)

DIXIE

I wish I was in de land of cotton,
Cinnamon seed and sandy bottom,
  Look away, look away, look away, Dixie land!
In Dixie land where I was born in,
Early on one frosty mornin',
  Look away, look away, away, Dixie land!

CHORUS

  Den I wish I was in Dixie, hooray, hooray!
  In Dixie's land we'll take our stand,
    To lib and die in Dixie.
  Away, away, away down South in Dixie!
  Away, away, away down South in Dixie!

Old Missus marry Will de weaber,
William was a gay deceaber;
  Look away, look away, look away, Dixie land!
And when he put his arm around her,
He look as fierce as a forty-pounder,
  Look away, look away, away, Dixie land!

His face was as sharp as a butcher's cleaber,
But dat did not seem to greab 'er;
  Look away, look away, look away, Dixie land!
Old Missus acted de foolest part,
And died for a man dat broke her heart,
  Look away, look away, away, Dixie land!

Now here's a health to de next old Missus,
An' all de gals dat want to kiss us,
  Look away, look away, look away, Dixie land!
But if you want to drive 'way sorrow,
Come and hear dis song to-morrow,
  Look away, look away, away, Dixie land!

Dar buckwheat-cakes and Injun batter,
Makes you fat or a little fatter,
  Look away, look away, look away, Dixie land!
Den hoe it down an' scratch your grabble,
To Dixie's land I'm bound to trabble,
  Look away, look away, away, Dixie land!

DANIEL EMMETT
(*Ohio*)

DEATH THE PEACEMAKER

The Blue and the Gray

A waste of land, a sodden plain,
  A lurid sunset sky,
With clouds that fled and faded fast
  In ghastly phantasy;
A field upturned by trampling feet,
  A field up-piled with slain,
With horse and rider blent in death
  Upon the battle-plain.

Two soldiers, lying as they fell
  Upon the reddened clay,
In daytime, foes; at night, in peace,
  Breathing their lives away.
Brave hearts had stirred each manly breast;
  Fate only made them foes;
And lying, dying, side by side,
  A softened feeling rose.

"Our time is short," one faint voice said.
  "Today we've done our best
On different sides. What matters now?
  Tomorrow we're at rest.
Life lies behind. I might not care
  For only my own sake;
But far away are other hearts
  That this day's work will break.

"Among New Hampshire's snowy hills
 There pray for me, tonight,
A woman and a little girl,
 With hair like golden light."
And at the thought broke forth, at last,
 The cry of anguish wild
That would no longer be repressed—
 "O God! my wife and child!"

"And," said the other dying man,
 "Across the Georgia plain
There watch and wait for me loved ones
 I'll never see again.
A little girl with dark bright eyes
 Each day waits at the door;
The father's step, the father's kiss,
 Will never meet her more.

"Today we sought each other's lives;
 Death levels all that now
For soon before God's mercy-seat
 Together we shall bow.
Forgive each other while we may;
 Life's but a weary game;
And right or wrong, the morning sun
 Will find us dead the same."

The dying lips the pardon breathe,
 The dying hands entwine;
The last ray dies, and over all
 The stars from heaven shine:
And the little girl with golden hair,
 And one with dark eyes bright,
On Hampshire's hills and Georgia Plain,
 Were fatherless that night.

ELLEN H. FLAGG
(*New Hampshire*)

SHERIDAN'S RIDE

Up from the South, at break of day,
Bringing to Winchester fresh dismay,
The affrighted air with a shudder bore,
Like a herald in haste to the chieftain's door,
The terrible grumble, and rumble, and roar,
Telling the battle was on once more,
  And Sheridan twenty miles away.

And wider still those billows of war
Thundered along the horizon's bar;
And louder yet into Winchester rolled
The roar of that red sea uncontrolled.
Making the blood of the listener cold,
As he thought of the stake in that fiery fray,
  With Sheridan twenty miles away.

But there is a road from Winchester town,
A good, broad highway leading down:
And there, through the flush of the morning light,
A steed as black as the steeds of night
Was seen to pass, as with eagle flight;
As if he knew the terrible need,
He stretched away with his utmost speed.
Hills rose and fell, but his heart was gay,
  With Sheridan fifteen miles away.

Still sprang from those swift hoofs, thundering south,
The dust like smoke from the cannon's mouth,
Or the trail of a comet, sweeping faster and faster,
Foreboding to traitors the doom of disaster.
The heart of the steed and the heart of the master
Were beating like prisoners assaulting their walls,
Impatient to be where the battle-field calls:
Every nerve of the charger was strained to full play,
  With Sheridan only ten miles away.

Under his spurning feet, the road
Like an arrowy Alpine river flowed,
And the landscape sped away behind
Like an ocean flying before the wind;
And the steed, like a bark fed with furnace ire,
Swept on, with his wild eye full of fire;
But, lo! he is nearing his heart's desire;
He is snuffing the smoke of the roaring fray,
With Sheridan only five miles away.

The first that the general saw were the groups
Of stragglers, and then the retreating troops;
What was done? what to do? a glance told him both.
Then striking his spurs with a terrible oath,
He dashed down the line, 'mid a storm of huzzas,
And the wave of retreat checked its course there, because
The sight of the master compelled it to pause.
With foam and with dust the black charger was gray:
By the flash of his eye, and the red nostril's play,
He seemed to the whole great army to say:
"I have brought you Sheridan all the way
From Winchester down to save the day."

Hurrah! hurrah for Sheridan!
Hurrah! hurrah for horse and man!
And when their statues are placed on high
Under the dome of the Union sky,
The American soldier's Temple of Fame,
There, with the glorious general's name,
Be it said, in letters both bold and bright:
"Here is the steed that saved the day
By carrying Sheridan into the fight,
From Winchester—twenty miles away!"

THOMAS BUCHANAN READ
(*Ohio*)

THE BATTLE AUTUMN OF 1862

The flags of war like storm-birds fly,
  The charging trumpets blow,
Yet rolls no thunder in the sky,
  No earthquake strives below.

And, calm and patient, Nature keeps
  Her ancient promise well,
Though o'er her bloom and greenness sweeps
  The battle's breath of hell.

And still she walks in golden hours
  Through harvest-happy farms,
And still she wears her fruits and flowers
  Like jewels on her arms.

What mean the gladness of the plain,
  This joy of eve and morn,
The mirth that shakes the beard of grain
  And yellow locks of corn?

Oh, eyes may be full of tears,
  And hearts with hate are hot;
But even-paced come round the years,
  And Nature changes not.

She meets with smiles our bitter grief,
  With songs our groans of pain;
She mocks with tint of flower and leaf
  The war-field's crimson stain.

Still, in the cannon's pause, we hear
  Her sweet thanksgiving-psalm;
Too near to God for doubt or fear,
  She shares the eternal calm.

She knows the seed lies safe below
The fires that blast and burn;
For all the tears of blood we sow
She waits the rich return.

She sees with clearer eye than ours
The good of suffering born—
The hearts that blossom like her flowers,
And ripen like her corn.

Oh, give to us, in times like these,
The vision of her eyes;
And make her fields and fruited trees
Our golden prophecies.

Oh, give to us her finer ear,
Above this stormy din.
We too would hear the bells of cheer
Ring peace and freedom in.

JOHN GREENLEAF WHITTIER
(*Massachusetts*)

THE SWORD OF ROBERT LEE

Forth from its scabbard, pure and bright,
Flashed the sword of Lee!
Far in the front of the deadly fight,
High o'er the brave in the cause of Right
Its stainless sheen, like a beacon light,
Led us to Victory!

Out of its scabbard, where, full long,
It slumbered peacefully,
Roused from its rest by the battle's song,
Shielding the feeble, smiting the strong,
Guarding the right, avenging the wrong,
Gleamed the sword of Lee!

Forth from its scabbard, high in air
  Beneath Virginia's sky—
And they who saw it gleaming there,
And knew who bore it, knelt to swear
That where that sword led they would dare
  To follow—and to die!

Out of its scabbard! Never hand
  Waved sword from stain as free,
Nor purer sword led braver band,
Nor braver bled for a brighter land,
Nor brighter land had a cause so grand,
  Nor cause a chief like Lee!

Forth from its scabbard! How we prayed
  That sword might victor be;
And when our triumph was delayed,
And many a heart grew sore afraid,
We still hoped on while gleamed the blade
  Of noble Robert Lee!

Forth from its scabbard all in vain
  Bright flashed the sword of Lee;
'Tis shrouded now in its sheath again,
It sleeps the sleep of our noble slain,
Defeated, yet without a stain,
  Proudly and peacefully!

ABRAM JOSEPH (FATHER) RYAN
(*Virginia*)

ASHBY

To the brave all homage render,
  Weep, ye skies of June!
With a radiance pure and tender,
  Shine, oh saddened moon!
"Dead upon the field of glory,"
Hero fit for song and story,
  Lies our bold dragoon.

Well they learned, whose hands have slain him,
  Braver, knightlier foe
Never fought with Moor nor Paynim,
  Rode at Templestowe,
With a mien how high and joyous,
'Gainst the hordes that would destroy us
  Went he forth we know.

Never more, alas! shall sabre
  Gleam around his crest;
Fought his fight; fulfilled his labor;
  Stilled his manly breast.
All unheard sweet Nature's cadence,
Trump of fame and voice of maidens,
  Now he takes his rest.

Earth, that all too soon hath bound him,
  Gently wrap his clay;
Linger lovingly around him,
  Light of dying day;
Softly fall the summer showers;
Birds and bees among the flowers
  Make the gloom seem gay.

There, throughout the coming ages,
  When his sword is rust,
And his deeds in classic pages,
  Mindful of her trust,
Shall Virginia, bending lowly,
Still a ceaseless vigil holy
  Keep above his dust!

John Reuben Thompson
(Virginia)

IN CAMP

I gazed forth from my wintry tent
  Upon the star-gemmed firmament;
I heard the far-off sentry's tramp
  Around our mountain-girdled camp,
And saw the ghostly tents uprise
  Like spectres 'neath the jeweled skies,
And thus upon the snow-clad scene,
  So pure and spotless and serene,
Where locked in sleep ten thousand lay
  Awaiting morn's returning ray,—
I gazed, till to the sun the drums
  Rolled at the dawn, "He comes, he comes."

William Heines Lytle
(*Ohio*)

THE SOUTHERN REPUBLIC

In the galaxy of nations,
  A nation's flag's unfurled,
Transcending in its martial pride
  The nations of the world.
Though born of war, baptized in blood,
  Yet mighty from the time,
Like fabled phoenix, forth she stood—
  Dismembered, yet sublime.

And braver heart, and bolder hand,
  Ne'er formed a fabric fair
As Southern wisdom can command,
  And Southern valor rear.
Though kingdoms scorn to own her sway,
  Or recognize her birth,
The land blood-bought for Liberty
  Will reign supreme on earth.

Clime of the Sun! Home of the Brave!
  Thy sons are bold and free,
And pour life's crimson tide to save
  Their birthright, Liberty!
Their fertile fields and sunny plains
  That yield the wealth alone,
That's coveted for greedy gains
  By despots—and a throne!

Proud country! battling, bleeding, torn,
  Thy altars desolate;
Thy lovely dark-eyed daughters mourn
  At war's relentless fate;
And widows' prayers, and orphans' tears,
  Her homes will consecrate,
While more than brass or marble rears
  The trophy of her great.

Oh! land that boasts each gallant name
  Of Jackson, Johnson, Lee,
And hosts of valiant sons, whose fame
  Extends beyond the sea;
Far rather let thy plains become,
  From gulf to mountain cave,
One honored sepulchre and tomb,
  Than we the tyrant's slave!

Fair, favored land! thou mayst be free,
  Redeemed by blood and war;
Through agony and gloom we see
  Thy hope—a glimmering star;
Thy banner, too, may proudly float,
  A herald on the seas—
Thy deeds of daring worlds remote
  Will emulate and praise!

But who can paint the impulse pure
That thrills and nerves thy grave
To deeds of valor, that secure
The rights their fathers gave?
Oh! grieve not, hearts; her matchless slain,
Crowned with the warrior's wreath,
From beds of fame their proud refrain
Was "Liberty or Death!"

Olivia Thomas
(*Mississippi*)

AT FREDERICKSBURG

(*December 13, 1862*)

God send us peace, and keep red strife away;
But should it come, God send us men of steel!
The land is dead that dare not face the day
When foreign danger threats the common weal.

Defenders strong are they that homes defend;
From ready arms the spoiler keeps afar.
Well blest the country that has sons to lend
From trades of peace to learn the trade of war.

Thrice blest the nation that has every son
A soldier, ready for the warning sound;
Who marches homeward when the fight is done,
To swing the hammer and to till the ground.

Call back that morning, with its lurid light,
When through our land the awful war-bell tolled;
When lips were mute, and women's faces white
As the pale cloud that out from Sumter rolled.

Call back that morn; an instant all were dumb
  As if the shot had struck the nation's life
Then cleared the smoke, and rolled the calling drum,
  And men streamed in to meet the coming strife.

They closed the ledger and they stilled the loom,
  The plough left rusting in the prairie farm;
They saw but "Union" in the gathering gloom;
  The tearless women helped the men to arm;

Brigades from towns—each village sent its band;
  German and Irish—every race and faith;
There was no question then of native land,
  But—love the Flag and follow it to death.

No need to tell their tale: through every age
  The splendid story shall be sung and said;
But let me draw one picture from the page
  For words of song embalm the hero dead.

The smooth hill is bare, and the cannons are planted,
Like Gorgon fates shading its terrible brow;
The word has been passed that the stormers are wanted.
And Burnside's battalions are mustering now.
The armies stand by to behold the dread meeting;
The work must be done by a desperate few;
The black-mouthed guns on the height give them greeting—
From gun-mouth to plain every grass blade in view.
Strong earthworks are there, and the rifles behind them
Are Georgia militia—and Irish brigade—
Their caps have green badges, as if to remind them
Of all the brave record their country has made.

The stormers go forward—the Federals cheer them;
They breast the smooth hillside—the black mouths are dumb;
The riflemen lie in the works till they near them,
And cover the stormers as upward they come.

Was ever a death-march so grand and so solemn?
At last, the dark summit with flame is enlined;
The great guns belch doom on the sacrificed column,
That reels from the height, leaving hundreds behind.
The armies are hushed—there is no cause for cheering:
The fall of brave men to brave men is a pain.
And again come the stormers! and as they are nearing
The flame-sheeted rifle-lines, reel back again.
And so till full noon come the Federal masses—
Flung back from the height, as the cliff flings a wave;
Brigade on brigade to the death-struggle passes,
No wavering rank till it steps on the grave.

Then comes a brief lull, and the smoke-pall is lifted
The green of the hillside no longer is seen;
The dead soldiers lie as the sea-weed is drifted,
The earthworks still held by the badges of green.
Have they quailed? is the word. No: again they are forming—
Again comes a column to death and defeat!
What is it in these who shall now do the storming
That makes every Georgian spring to his feet?

"O God! What a pity!" they cry in their cover,
As rifles are readied and bayonets made tight:
"'Tis Meagher and his fellows! their caps have green clover;
'Tis Greek to Greek now for the rest of the fight!"
Twelve hundred the column, their rent flag before them,
With Meagher at their head, they have dashed at the hill!
Their foemen are proud of the country that bore them;
But, Irish in love, they are enemies still.
Out rings the fierce word, "Let them have it!" the rifles
Are emptied point-blank in the hearts of the foe;
It is green against green, but a principle stifles
The Irishman's love in the Georgian's blow
The column has reeled, but it is not defeated; in front of the guns they re-form and attack;

Six times they have done it, and six times retreated;
Twelve hundred they came, and two hundred go back.
Two hundred go back with the chivalrous story;
The wild day is closed in the night's solemn shroud;
A thousand lie dead, but their death is a glory
That calls not for tears—the Green Badges are proud!

Bright honor be theirs who for honor were fearless,
Who charged for their flag to the grim cannon's mouth;
And honor to them who were true, though not tearless
Who bravely that day kept the cause of the South.
The quarrel is done—God avert such another;
The lesson it brought we should evermore heed;
Who loveth the Flag is a man and a brother,
No matter what birth or what race or what creed.

JOHN BOYLE O'REILLY
(*Massachusetts*)

HONORS OF WAR

On the death of Ephraim E. Ellsworth, shot at Alexandria, Va., May 24, 1861

Wails of slow music move along the street,
Before the slow march of a myriad feet
  Whose mournful echoes come;
Banners are muffled, hiding all their sight
Of sacred stars—the century's dearest light—
  And, muffled, throbs the drum.

Proud is the hearse our Mother gives her son,
On the red altar laid her earliest one,
  Wrapp'd in her holiest pall
He goes: her household guardians follow him;
Eyes with their new heroic tears are dim;
  The stern tomorrows call:

Well might the youth who saw his coffined face,
Lying in state within the proudest place,
  Long for a lot so high;
He was the first to leap the treacherous wall;
First in the arms of Death and Fame to fall—
  To live because to die.

Pass on, with wails of music, moving slow,
The dark dead-march, O Mother dress'd in woe.
  Lo, many another way
Shall blacken after, many a sacred head
Brightly thy stares shall fold, alive though dead,
  From many a funeral day.

Weep, but grow stronger in thy suffering:
From their dead brothers' graves thy sons shall bring
  New life of love for thee:
The long death-marches herald, slow or fast,
The resurrection-hour of men at last
  New-born in Liberty.

JOHN JAMES PIATT
(Ohio)

O CAPTAIN, MY CAPTAIN

O Captain, my Captain, our fearful trip is done,
The ship has weather'd every rack, the prize we sought is won,
The port is near, the bells I hear, the people all exulting,
While follow eyes the steady keel, the vessel grim and daring;
  But O heart, heart, heart,
    O the bleeding drops of red,
      Where on the deck my Captain lies,
        Fallen cold and dead.

O Captain, my Captain, rise up and hear the bells;
Rise up—for you the flag is flung—for you the bugle trills,

For you bouquets and ribbon'd wreaths—for you the shores
 a-crowding,
For you they call, the swaying mass, their eager faces turning;
 Here Captain, dear father,
 This arm beneath your head,
 It is some dream that on the deck
 You've fallen cold and dead.

My Captain does not answer, his lips are pale and still,
My father does not feel my arm, he has no pulse nor will,
The ship is anchor'd safe and sound, its voyage closed and done,
From fearful trip the victor ship comes in with object won;
 Exult O shores, and ring O bells,
 But I, with mournful tread,
 Walk the deck my Captain lies,
 Fallen cold and dead.

WALT WHITMAN
(*New York*)

MARCHING THROUGH GEORGIA

Bring the good old bugle, boys, we'll sing another song—
Sing it with a spirit that will start the world along—
Sing it as we used to sing it fifty thousand strong,
While we were marching through Georgia.

CHORUS

"Hurrah! Hurrah! we bring the jubilee!
Hurrah! Hurrah! the flag that makes you free!"
So we sang the chorus from Atlanta to the sea,
While we were marching through Georgia.

How the darkeys shouted when they heard the joyful sound!
How the turkeys gobbled which our commissary found!
How the sweet potatoes even started from the ground,
While we were marching through Georgia.

Yes, and there were Union men who wept with joyful tears,
When they saw the honored flag they had not seen for years;
Hardly could they be restrained from breaking forth in cheers,
While we were marching through Georgia.

"Sherman's dashing Yankee boys will never reach the coast!"
So the saucy rebels said—and 'twas a handsome boast,
Had they not forgot, alas! to reckon on a host,
While we were marching through Georgia.

So we made a thoroughfare for Freedom and her train,
Sixty miles in latitude—three hundred to the main;
Treason fled before us, for resistance was in vain,
While we were marching through Georgia.

HENRY CLAY WORK

THOMAS AT CHICKAMAUGA

It was that fierce contested field when Chickamauga lay
Beneath the wild tornado that swept her pride away;
Her dimpling dales and circling hills dyed crimson with the flood
That had its sources in the springs that throb with human blood.

"Go say to General Hooker to reinforce his right!"
Said Thomas to his aide-de-camp, when wildly went the fight;
In front the battle thundered, it roared both right and left,
But like a rock "Pap" Thomas stood upon the crested cleft.

"Where will I find you, General, when I return?" The aide
Leaned on his bridle-rein to wait the answer Thomas made;
The old chief like a lion turned, his pale lips set and sere,
And shook his mane, and stamped his foot, and fiercely answered,
"Here!"

The floodtide of fraternal strife rolled upward to his feet,
And like the breakers on the shore the thunderous clamors beat;
The sad earth rocked and reeled with woe, the woodland shrieked
in pain,
And hill and vale were groaning with the burden of the slain.

Who does not mind that sturdy form, that steady heart and hand,
That calm repose and gallant mien, that courage high and grand?—
O God, who givest nations men to meet their lofty needs,
Vouchsafe another Thomas when our country prostrate bleeds!

They fought with all the fortitude of earnest men and true—
The men who wore the rebel gray, the men who wore the blue;
And those, they fought most valiantly for petty state and clan,
And these, for truer Union and the brotherhood of man.

They come, those hurling legions, with banners crimson-splashed,
Against our stubborn columns their rushing ranks are dashed,
Till 'neath the blistering iron hail the shy and frightened deer
Go scurrying from their forest haunts to plunge in wilder fear.

Beyond, our lines are broken: and now in frenzied rout
The flower of the Cumberland has swiftly faced about;
And horse and foot and color-guard are reeling, rear and van,
And in the awful panic man forgets that he is man.

Now Bragg, with pride exultant above our broken wings,
The might of all his army against "Pap" Thomas brings;
They're massing to the right of him, they're massing to the left,
Ah, God be with our hero, who holds the crested cleft!

Blow, blow, ye echoing bugles! give answer, screaming shell!
Go, belch your murderous fury, ye batteries of hell!
Ring out, O impious musket! spin on, O shattering shot,—
Our smoke-encircled hero, he hears but heeds ye not!

Now steady, men! now steady! make one more valiant stand,
For gallant Steedman's coming, his forces well in hand!
Close up your shattered columns, take steady aim and true,
The chief who loves you as his life will live or die with you!

By solid columns, on they come; by columns they are hurled,
As down the eddying rapids the storm-swept booms are whirled;
And when the ammunition fails—O moment drear and dread—
The heroes load their blackened guns from rounds of soldiers dead.

God never set His signet on the hearts of braver men,
Or fixed the goal of victory on higher heights than then;
With bayonets and muskets clubbed, they close the rush and roar;
Their stepping-stones to glory are their comrades gone before.

O vanished majesty of days not all forgotten yet,
We consecrate unto thy praise one hour of deep regret;
One hour to them whose days were years of glory that shall flood
The Nation's sombre night of tears, of carnage, and of blood!

O vanished majesty of days, when men were gauged by worth,
Set crowned and dowered in the way to judge the sons of earth;
When all the little great fell down before the great unknown,
And priest put off the hampering gown and coward donned his own!

O vanished majesty of days that saw the sun shine on
The deeds that wake sublimer praise than Ghent or Marathon;
When patriots in homespun rose—where one was called for, ten—
And heroes sprang full-armored from the humblest walks of men!

O vanished majesty of days! Rise, type and mould today,
And teach our sons to follow on where duty leads the way;
That whatsoever trial comes, defying doubt and fear,
They in the thickest fight shall stand and proudly answer, "Here"!

KATE BROWNLEE SHERWOOD

ASHES OF GLORY

Fold up the gorgeous silken sun,
  By blending martyrs blest,
And heap the laurels it has won
  Above its place of rest.

No trumpet's note need harshly blare—
  No drum funereal roll—
No trailing sables drape the bier
  That frees a dauntless soul.

It lived with Lee, and decked his brow
  With fate's empyreal Palm
It sleeps the sleep of Jackson now—
  As spotless and as calm.

It was outnumbered—not outdone;
  And they shall shuddering tell
Who struck the blow, its latest gun
  Flashed ruin as it fell.

Sleep, shrouded ensign! Not the breeze
  That smote the victor tar
With death across the heaving seas
  Of fiery Trafalgar;

Not Arthur's Knights amid the gloom
  Their knightly deeds have starred;
Nor Gallic Henry's matchless plume,
  Nor peerless-born Bayard;

Not all that antique fables feign,
  And orient dreams disgorge;
Not yet the silver cross of Spain,
  And Lion of St. George,

Can bid thee pale! Proud emblem, still
Thy crimson glory shines
Beyond the lengthened shades that fill
Their proudest kingly lines.

Sleep! in thine own historic night—
And be thy blazoned scroll;
A warrior's banner takes its flight
To greet the warrior's soul.

AUGUSTUS JULIAN REQUIER
(*Alabama*)

LITTLE GIFFEN

Out of the focal and foremost fire,
Out of the hospital walls as dire,
Smitten of grape-shot and gangrene
(Eighteenth battle and he sixteen)—
Spectre such as you seldom see,
Little Giffen of Tennessee.

"Take him—and welcome!" the surgeons said,
"Little the doctor can help the dead!"
So we took him and brought him where
The balm was sweet on the summer air;
And we laid him down on a wholesome bed—
Utter Lazarus, heel to head!

And we watched the war with bated breath—
Skeleton Boy against skeleton Death.
Months of torture, how many such!
Weary weeks of the stick and crutch;
And still a glint in the steel-blue eye
Told of a spirit that wouldn't die.

And didn't. Nay, more! in death's despite
The crippled skeleton learned to write.
"Dear Mother," at first, of course; and then

"Dear Captain," inquiring about "the men."
Captain's answer: "Of eighty and five,
Giffen and I are left alive."

Word of gloom from the war one day:
"Johnston's pressed at the front, they say!"
Little Giffen was up and away;
A tear—his first—as he bade good-by,
Dimmed the glint of his steel-blue eye.
"I'll write, if spared!" There was news of the fight:
But none of Giffen—he did not write.

I sometimes fancy that, were I king
Of the princely knights of the Golden Ring,
With the song of the minstrel in mine ear,
And the tender legend that trembles here,
I'd give the best, on his bended knee,
The whitest soul of my chivalry,
For Little Giffen of Tennessee.

FRANCIS ORRERY TICKNOR

MANASSAS

They have met at last—as storm-clouds
        Meet in heaven,
And the Northmen back and bleeding
        Have been driven;
And their thunders have been stilled,
And their leaders crushed or killed,
And their ranks with terror thrilled,
        Rent and riven!

Like the leaves of Valambrosa
        They are lying;
In the moonlight, in the midnight,
        Dead and dying;

Like those leaves before the gale,
Swept their legions, wild and pale;
While the host that made them quail
    Stood, defying.

When aloft in morning sunlight
    Flags were flaunted,
And "swift vengeance on the rebel"
    Proudly vaunted:
Little did they think that night
Should close upon their shameful flight,
And rebels, victors in the fight,
    Stand undaunted.

But peace to those who perished
    In our passes!
Light be the earth above them;
    Green the grasses!
Long shall Northmen rue the day
When they met our stern array,
And shrunk from battle's wild affray
    At Manassas.

Catherine M. Warfield

STONEWALL JACKSON'S WAY

Come, stack arms, men; pile on the rails;
  Stir up the camp-fire bright!
No growling if the canteen fails;
  We'll make a roaring night.
Here Shenandoah brawls along,
Here burly Blue Ridge echoes strong,
To swell the brigade's rousing song,
  Of "Stonewall Jackson's way."

We see him now—the queer slouch hat
  Cocked o'er his eye askew;
The shrewd, dry smile; the speech so pat,
  So calm, so blunt, so true.
The "Bluelight Elder" knows 'em well;
Says he, "That's Banks; he's fond of shell.
Lord, save his soul! We'll give him"—well,
  That's Stonewall Jackson's way.

Silence! Ground arms! Kneel all! Caps off!
  Old Massa's going to pray.
Strangle the fool that dares to scoff.
  Attention! it's his way.
Appealing from his native sod,
In forma pauperis to God,
"Lay bare thine arm! Stretch forth thy rod.
  Amen." That's Stonewall's way.

He's in the saddle now. Fall in,
  Steady the whole brigade!
Hill's at the ford, cut off; we'll win
  His way out, ball and blade.
What matter if our shoes are worn?
What matter if our feet are torn?
Quick step! We're with him before morn—
  That's Stonewall Jackson's way.

The sun's bright lances rout the mists
  Of morning; and, by George!
Here's Longstreet, struggling in the lists,
  Hemmed in an ugly gorge.
Pope and his Dutchmen! whipped before.
"Bay'nets and grape!" hear Stonewall roar.
Charge, Stuart! Pay off Ashby's score
  In Stonewall Jackson's way.

Ah! maiden, wait and watch and yearn
  For news of Stonewall's band.
Ah! widow, read with eyes that burn
  That ring upon thy hand.
Ah! wife, sew on, pray on, hope on;
Thy life shall not be all forlorn;
The foe had better ne'er been born
  That gets in Stonewall's way.

JOHN WILLIAMSON PALMER

ALABAMA

Alabama, Alabama,
  We will aye be true to thee,
From thy Southern shore where groweth,
  By the sea thy orange tree,
To thy Northern vale where floweth
  Deep and blue thy Tennessee,
Alabama, Alabama,
  We will aye be true to thee!

Broad the stream whose name thou bearest;
  Grand thy Bigbee rolls along;
Fair thy Coosa—Tallapoosa;
  Bold thy Warrior, dark and strong;
Goodlier than the land that Moses
  Climbed lone Nebo's Mount to see,
Alabama, Alabama,
  We will aye be true to thee!

From thy prairies broad and fertile,
  Where the snow-white cotton shines,
To the hills where coal and iron
  Hide in thy exhaustless mines,
Strong-armed miners—sturdy farmers;
  Loyal hearts whate'er we be,
Alabama, Alabama,
  We will aye be true to thee!

From thy quarries where the marble
  White as that of Paros gleams,
Waiting 'till thy sculptor's chisel
  Wake to life thy poet's dreams;
For not only wealth of nature,
  Wealth of mind hast thou in fee,
Alabama, Alabama,
  We will aye be true to thee!

Where the perfumed south-wind whispers,
  Thy magnolia groves among,
Softer than a mother's kisses,
  Sweeter than a mother's song;
Where the golden jasmine trailing,
  Woos the treasure-laden bee,
Alabama, Alabama,
  We will aye be true to thee!

Brave and pure thy men and women,
  Better this than corn and wine,
Make us worthy, God in heaven,
  Of this goodly land of thine;
Hearts as open as our doorways,
  Liberal hands and spirits free,
Alabama, Alabama,
  We will aye be true to thee!

Little, little, can I give thee,
  Alabama, mother mine;
But that little—hand, brain, spirit—
  All I have and am are thine,
Take, O take, the gift and giver,
  Take and serve thyself with me,
Alabama, Alabama,
  I will aye be true to thee!

JULIA TUTWILER
(*Alabama*)

CAROLINA

I

The despot treads thy sacred sands,
Thy pines give shelter to his bands
Thy sons stand by with idle hands
Carolina!
He breathes at ease thy airs of balm,
He scorns the lances of thy palm;
Oh! who shall break thy craven calm,
Carolina!
Thy ancient fame is growing dim,
A spot is on thy garment's rim;
Give to the winds thy battle hymn,
Carolina!

II

Call thy children of the hill,
Wake swamp and river, coast and rill,
Rouse all thy strength and all thy skill,
Carolina!
Cite wealth and science, trade and art,
Touch with thy fire the cautious mart,
And pour thee through the people's heart,
Carolina!
Till even the coward spurns his fears,
And all thy fields and fens and meres
Shall bristle like thy palm with spears,
Carolina!

III

Hold up the glories of thy dead;
Say how thy elder children bled,
And point to Eutaw's battle bed,
Carolina!

Tell how the patriot's soul was tried,
And what his dauntless breast defied;
How Rutledge ruled and Laurens died,
Carolina!
Cry! till thy summons, heard at last,
Shall fall like Marion's bugle-blast
Re-echoed from the haunted Past,
Carolina!

IV

I hear a murmur as of waves
That grope their way through sunless caves,
Like bodies struggling in their graves,
Carolina!
And now it deepens; slow and grand
It swells, as rolling to the land,
An ocean broke upon the strand,
Carolina!
Shout! let it reach the startled Huns!
And roar with all thy festal guns!
It is the answer of thy sons,
Carolina!

V

They will not wait to hear thee call;
From Sachem's Head to Sumter's wall
Resounds the voice of hut and hall,
Carolina!
No! thou hast not a stain, they say,
Or none save what the battle-day
Shall wash in seas of blood away,
Carolina!
Thy skirts indeed the foe may part,
Thy robe be pierced with sword and dart,
They shall not touch thy noble heart,
Carolina!

VI

Ere thou shalt own the tyrant's thrall
Ten times ten thousand men must fall;
Thy corpse may hearken to his call,
Carolina!
When, by thy bier, in mournful throngs
The women chant thy mortal wrongs,
'Twill be their own funereal songs,
Carolina!
From thy dead breast by ruffians trod
No helpless child shall look to God;
All shall be safe beneath thy sod,
Carolina!

VII

Girt with such wills to do and bear,
Assured in right, and mailed in prayer.
Thou wilt not bow thee to despair,
Carolina!
Throw thy bold banner to the breeze!
Front with thy ranks the threatening seas
Like thine own proud armorial trees,
Carolina!
Fling down thine gauntlet to the Huns,
And roar the challenge from thy guns;
Then leave the future to thy sons,
Carolina!

HENRY TIMROD

CIVIL WAR

"Rifleman, shoot me a fancy shot
  Straight at the heart of yon prowling vidette;
Ring me a ball in the glittering spot
  That shines on his breast like an amulet!"

"Ah, captain! here goes for a fine-drawn bead,
  There's music around when my barrel's in tune!"
Crack! went the rifle, the messenger sped,
  And dead from his horse fell the ringing dragoon.

"Now, rifleman, steal through the bushes, and snatch
  From your victim some trinket to handsel first blood;
A button, a loop, or that luminous patch
  That gleams in the moon like a diamond stud!"

"O captain! I staggered, and sunk on my track,
  When I gazed on the face of that fallen vidette,
For he looked so like you, as he lay on his back,
  That my heart rose upon me, and masters me yet.

"But I snatched off the trinket,—this locket of gold;
  An inch from the centre my lead broke its way,
Scarce grazing the picture, so fair to behold,
  Of a beautiful lady in bridal array."

"Ha! rifleman, fling me the locket!—'tis she.
  My brother's young bride, and the fallen dragoon
Was her husband—Hush! soldier, 't was Heaven's decree,
  We must bury him there, by the light of the moon!

"But, hark! the far bugles their warnings unite;
  War is a virtue—weakness a sin;
There's a lurking and loping around us tonight;
  Load again, rifleman, keep your hand in!"

CHARLES DAWSON SHANLY

SOMEBODY'S DARLING

Into a ward of the whitewashed halls
  Where the dead and dying lay,
Wounded by bayonets, shells and balls,
  Somebody's darling was borne one day.
Somebody's darling, so young and brave,
  Wearing still on his pale sweet face—
Soon to be hid by the dust of the grave—
  The lingering light of his boyhood's grace.

Matted and damp are the curls of gold
  Kissing the snow of that fair young brow;
Pale are the lips of delicate mould,
  Somebody's darling is dying now.
Back from the beautiful blue-veined brow
  Brush every wandering silken thread.
Cross his hands on his bosom now—
  Somebody's darling is still and dead!

Kiss him once for somebody's sake;
  Murmur a prayer both soft and low;
One bright curl from its fair mates take—
  They were somebody's pride, you know.
Somebody's hand has rested there;
  Was it a mother's, soft and white?
Or have the lips of a sister fair
  Been baptized in those waves of light?

God knows best! He was somebody's love;
  Somebody's heart enshrined him there—
Somebody wafted his name above,
  Night and morn, on the wings of prayer.
Somebody wept when he marched away,
  Looking so handsome, brave and grand;
Somebody's kiss on his forehead lay,
  Somebody clung to his parting hand.

Somebody's watching and waiting for him,
  Yearning to hold him again to her heart;
And there he lies—with his blue eyes dim,
  And the smiling, childlike lips apart.
Tenderly bury the fair young dead,
  Pausing to drop on his grave a tear;
Carve on the wooden slab o'er his head,
  "Somebody's darling slumbers here."

MARIE LA COSTE

THE BONNIE BLUE FLAG

We are a band of brothers
  And native to the soil,
Fighting for the property
  We gained by honest toil;
And when our rights were threatened,
  The cry rose near and far—
"Hurrah for the Bonnie Blue Flag
  That bears the single star"

CHORUS

Hurrah! hurrah!
  For Southern rights, hurrah!
Hurrah for the Bonnie Blue Flag
  That bears the single star.

As long as the Union
  Was faithful to her trust,
Like friends and like brothers
  Both kind were we and just;
But now, when Northern treachery
  Attempts our rights to mar,
We hoist on high the Bonnie Blue Flag
  That bears the single star.

CHORUS

First gallant South Carolina
  Nobly made the stand,

Then came Alabama,
Who took her by the hand;
Next quickly Mississippi,
Georgia and Florida
All raised on high the Bonnie Blue Flag,
That bears the single star.
CHORUS

And here's to old Virginia—
The Old Dominion State—
With the young Confed'racy
At length has linked her fate,
Impelled by her example,
Now other states prepare
To hoist on high the Bonnie Blue Flag
That bears the single star.
CHORUS

Then here's to our Confed'racy,
Strong are we and brave,
Like patriots of old we'll fight
Our heritage to save.
And rather than submit to shame,
To die we would prefer;
So cheer for the Bonnie Blue Flag
That bears the single star.
CHORUS

Then cheer, boys, cheer;
Raise the joyous shout,
For Arkansas and North Carolina
Now have both gone out;
And let another rousing cheer
For Tennessee be given,
The single star of the Bonnie Blue Flag
Has grown to be eleven.
CHORUS

HARRY MCCARTHY

WE'RE TENTING TONIGHT

We're tenting tonight on the old camp ground,
Give us a song to cheer our weary hearts,
A song of home,
And friends we love so dear.

We've been tenting tonight on the old camp ground,
Thinking of days gone by,
Of the loved ones at home that gave us the hand,
And the tear that said "good-bye"

We are tired of war on the old camp ground,
Many are dead and gone,
Of the brave and true who've left their homes,
Others been wounded long.

We've been fighting today on the old camp ground,
Many are lying near;
Some are dead and some are dying,
Many are in tears.

Many are the hearts that are weary tonight,
Wishing for the war to cease;
Many are the hearts looking for the right,
To see the dawn of peace.

Tenting tonight,
Tenting tonight,
Tenting on the old camp ground,
Dying tonight,
Dying on the old camp ground.

WALTER KITTREDGE

ONLY ONE KILLED

Only one killed—in company B
  'Twas a trifling loss—one man!
A charge of the bold and dashing Lee—
While merry enough it was to see
  The enemy, as he ran.

Only one killed upon our side—
  Once more to the field they turn.
Quietly now the horsemen ride—
And pause by the form of the one who died
  So bravely, as now we learn.

Their grief for the comrade loved and true
  For a time was unconcealed;
They saw the bullet had pierced him through,
That his pain was brief—ah! very few
  Die thus, on the battle-field.

The news has gone to his home, afar—
  Of the short and gallant fight,
Of the noble deeds of the young La Var
Whose life went out as a falling star
  In the skirmish of that night.

"Only one killed! It was my son,"
  The widowed mother cried.
She turned but to clasp the sinking one,
  Who heard not the words of the victory won,
  But of him who had bravely died.

Ah! death to her were a sweet relief,
  The bride of a single year.
Oh, would she might, with her weight of grief,
Lie down in the dust, with the autumn leaf
  Now trodden and brown and sere!

But no, she must bear through coming life
  Her burden of silent woe,
The aged mother and youthful wife
Must live through a nation's bloody strife,
  Sighing and waiting to go.

Where the loved are meeting beyond the stars,
  Are meeting no more to part.
They can smile once more through the crystal bars—
Where never more will the woe of wars
  O'ershadow the loving heart.

JULIA L. KEYES

WHAT THE VILLAGE BELL SAID

Full many a year in the village church,
  Above the world have I made my home;
And happier there, than if I had hung
  High up in the air in a golden dome;
    For I have tolled
    When the slow hearse rolled
  Its burden sad to my door;
    And each echo that woke,
    With the solemn stroke,
  Was a sigh from the heart of the poor.

I know the great bell of the city spire
  Is a far prouder one than such as I;
And its deafening stroke, compared with mine,
  Is thunder compared with a sigh:
    But the shattering note
    Of his brazen throat,
  As it swells on the Sabbath air,
    Far oftener rings
    For other things
  Than a call to the house of prayer.

Brave boy, I tolled when your father died,
And you wept while my tones pealed loud;
And more gently I rung when the lily-white dame,
Your mother dear, lay in her shroud:
And I sang in sweet tone
The angels might own,
When your sister you gave to your friend;
Oh! I rang with delight,
On that sweet summer night,
When they vowed they would love to the end!

But a base foe comes from the regions of crime,
With a heart all hot with the flames of hell;
And the tones of the bell you have loved so long
No more on the air shall swell:
For the people's chief,
With his proud belief
That his country's cause is God's own,
Would change the song,
The hills have rung,
To the thunder's harsher tone.

Then take me down from the village church,
Where in peace so long I have hung;
But I charge you, by all the loved and lost,
Remember the songs I have sung
Remember the mound
Of holy ground,
Where your father and mother lie;
And swear by the love
For the dead above
To beat your foul foe or die.

Then take me; but when (I charge you this)
  You have come to the bloody field,
That the bell of God, to a cannon grown,
  You will ne'er to the foeman yield.
    By the love of the past,
    Be that hour your last,
  When the foe has reached this trust;
    And make him a bed
    Of patriot dead,
  And let him sleep in this holy dust.

JOHN G. M'LEMORE

THE BATTLE RAINBOW

The warm, weary day was departing—the smile
  Of the sunset gave token the tempest had ceased;
And the lightning yet fitfully gleamed for a while
  On the cloud that sank sullen and dark in the east.

There our army—awaiting the terrible fight
  Of the morrow—lay hopeful and watching, and still;
Where their tents all the region had sprinkled with white,
  From river to river, o'er meadow and hill.

While above them the fierce cannonade of the sky
  Blazed and burst from the vapors that muffled the sun,
Their "counterfeit clamors" gave forth no reply;
  And slept till the battle, the charge in each gun.

When, lo! on the cloud, a miraculous thing!
  Broke in beauty the rainbow our hosts to enfold;
The centre o'erspread by its arch, and each wing
  Suffused with its azure and crimson and gold.

Blest omen of victory, symbol divine
  Of peace after tumult, repose after pain;
How sweet and how glowing with promise the sign,
  To eyes that should never behold it again!

For the fierce flame of war on the morrow flashed out,
  And its thunder-peals filled all the tremulous air:
Over slippery intrenchment and reddened redoubt,
  Rang the wild cheer of triumph, the cry of despair.

Then a long week of glory and agony came—
  Of mute supplication, and yearning, and dread;
When day unto day gave the record of fame,
  And night unto night gave the list of its dead.

We had triumphed—the foe had fled back to his ships—
  His standard in rags and his legions a wreck—
But alas! the stark faces and colorless lips
  Of our loved ones, gave triumph's rejoicing a check.

And yet, oh, not yet, as a sign of release,
  Had the Lord set in mercy His bow in the cloud;
Not yet had the Comforter whispered of peace
  To the hearts that around us lay bleeding and bowed.

But the promise was given—the beautiful arc,
  With its brilliant profusion of colors, that spanned
The sky on that exquisite eve, was the mark
  Of the Infinite Love overarching the land.

And that Love, shining richly and full as the day,
  Through the tear-drops that moisten each martyr's proud pall,
On the gloom of the past the bright bow shall display
  Of Freedom, Peace, Victory, bent over all.

JOHN R. THOMPSON
(Virginia)

GRAVE OF ALBERT SIDNEY JOHNSTON

The Lone Star State secretes the clay
  Of him who led on Shiloh's field,
Where mourning wives will stop to pray,
  And maids a weeping tribute yield.

In after time, when spleen and strife
  Their madd'ning flame shall have expired,
The noble deeds that gemm'd this life
  By Age and Youth will be admired.

As o'er the stream the boatmen rove
  By Pittsburg Bend at early Spring,
They'll show with moist'ning eye the grave
  Where havoc spread her sable wing.

There, 'neath the budding foliage green,
  Ere Night evolved her dewy breath,
While Vict'ry smiled upon the scene,
  Our Chieftain met the blow of death.

Great men to come will bless the brave;
  The soldier, bronzed in War's career,
Shall weave a chaplet o'er his grave,
  While Mem'ry drops the glist'ning tear.

Though envy wag her scorpion tongue,
  The march of Time shall find his fame;
Where Bravery's loved and Glory's sung,
  There children's lips shall lisp his name.

J. B. Synnott
(*Texas*)

OVER THE RIVER

We hail your "Stripes" and lessened "Stars,"
  As one may hail a neighbor;
Now forward move! no fear of jars,
  With nothing but free labor;
And we will mind our slaves and farm,
And never wish you any harm,
  But greet you—over the river.

The self-same language do we speak,
  The same dear words we utter;
Then let's not make each other weak,
  Nor 'gainst each other mutter;
But let each go his separate way,
And each will doff his hat, and say:
  "I greet you—over the river!"

Our flags, almost the same, unfurl,
  And nod across the border;
Ohio's waves between them curl—
  Our stripe's a little broader;
May yours float out on every breeze,
And, in our wake, traverse all seas—
  We greet you—over the river!

We part as friends of years should part,
  With pleasant words and wishes,
And no desire is in our heart
  For Lincoln's loaves and fishes:
"Farewell," we wave you from afar,
We like you best—just where you are—
  And greet you—over the river!

JANE T. H. CROSS

A BALLAD OF THE WAR

Watchman, what of the night?
  Through the city's darkening street,
Silent and slow the guardsmen go
    On their long and lonely beat.

Darkly, drearily down
  Falleth the wintry rain;
And the cold, gray mist hath the roof-tops kissed,
  As it glides o'er town and plain.

Beating against the windows,
  The sleet falls heavy and chill,
And the children draw nigher 'round hearth and fire,
  As the blast shrieks loud and shrill.

Silent is all without,
  Save the sentry's challenge grim,
And a hush sinks down o'er the weary town,
  And the sleeper's eyes are dim.

Watchman, what of the night?
  Hark! from the old church-tower
Rings loud and clear on the misty air,
  The chime of the midnight hour.

But another sound breaks in,
  A summons deep and rude,
The roll of the drum, and the rush and hum
  Of a gathering multitude.

And the dim and flickering torch
  Sheds a red and lurid glare,
O'er the long dark line, whose bayonets shine
  Faintly, yet sternly there.

A low, deep voice is heard:
  "Rest on your arms, my men."
Then the muskets clank through each serried rank,
  And all is still again.

Pale faces and tearful eyes
  Gaze down on that grim array,
For a rumor hath spread that that column dread
  Marcheth ere break of day.

Marcheth against "the rebels,"
  Whose camp lies heavy and still,
Where the driving sleet and cold rain beat
  On the brow of a distant hill.

And the mother's heart grows faint,
  As she thinks of her darling one,
Who perchance may lie 'neath that wintry sky,
  Ere the long, dark night be done.

Pallid and haggard, too,
  Is the cheek of the fair young wife;
And her eyes grow dim as she thinks of him
  She loveth more than life.

For fathers, husbands, sons,
  Are the "rebels" the foe would smite,
And earnest the prayer for those lives so dear,
  And a bleeding country's right.

And where their treasure is,
  There is each loving heart;
And sadly they gaze by the torches' blaze,
  And the tears unbidden start.

Is there none to warn the camp,
None from that anxious throng?
Ah, the rain beats down o'er plain and town—
The way is dark and long.

No man is left behind,
None that is brave and true,
And the bayonets, bright in the lurid light
With menace stern shine through.

Guarded is every street,
Brutal the hireling foe;
Is there one heart here will boldly dare
So brave a deed to do?

Look! in her still, dark room,
Alone a woman kneels,
With Care's deep trace on her pale, worn face,
And Sorrow's ruthless seals.

Wrinkling her placid brow,
A matron, she, and fair,
Though wan her cheek, and the silver streak
Gemming her glossy hair.

A moment in silent prayer
Her pale lips move, and then,
Through the dreary night, like an angel bright,
On her mission of love to men.

She glideth upon her way,
Through the lonely, misty street,
Shrinking with dread as she hears the tread
Of the watchman on his beat.

Onward, aye, onward still,
  Far past the weary town,
Till languor doth seize on her feeble knees,
  And the heavy hands hang down.

But bravely she struggles on,
  Breasting the cold, dank rain,
And, heavy and chill, the mist from the hill
  Sweeps down upon the plain.

Hark! far behind she hears
  A dull and muffled tramp,
But before her the gleam of the watch-fire's beam
  Shines out from the Southern camp.

She hears the sentry's challenge,
  Her work of love is done;
She has fought a good fight, and on Fame's proud height
  Hath a crown of glory won.

Oh, they tell of a Tyrol maiden,
  Who saved from a ruthless foe
Her own fair town, 'mid its mountains brown,
  Three hundred years ago.

And I've read in tales heroic
  How a noble Scottish maid
Her own life gave, her king to save
  From the foul assassin's blade.

But if these, on the rolls of honor,
  Shall live in lasting fame,
Oh, close beside, in grateful pride,
  We'll write this matron's name.

And when our fair-haired children
  Shall cluster round our knee,
With wondering gaze, as we tell of the days
  When we swore that we would be free.

We'll tell them the thrilling story,
  And we'll say to each childish heart,
"By this gallant deed, at thy country's need,
  Be ready to do thy part."

GEORGE HERBERT SASS

THROUGH FIRE IN MOBILE BAY

1864

I'd weave a wreath for those who fought
  In blue upon the wave,
I drop a tear for all who sleep
  Down in the coral caves,
And proudly do I touch my cap
  Whene'er I meet today
A man who sail'd with Farragut
  Thro' fire in Mobile Bay.

Oh what a gallant sight it was
  As toward the foe we bore,
Lashed to the mast, unflinching stood
  Our grand old Commodore,
I see him now above the deck,
  Though time has cleared away
The battle smoke that densely hung
  Above old Mobile Bay.

Torpedoes to the right and left,
  Torpedoes straight ahead,
The stanch Tecumseh sinks from sight,
  The waves receive her dead.

But on we press thro' lead and iron,
  On, on with pennons gay,
Whilst glory holds her wreath above
  Immortal Mobile Bay.

The rebel forts belch fire and death,
  But what care we for them?
Our onward course with Farragut
  To guide us, naught can stem.
The Hartford works her dreaded guns,
  The Brooklyn pounds away,
And proudly flies the flag of stars
  Aloft o'er Mobile Bay.

Behold yon moving mass of iron
  Beyond the Ossipee;
To fight the fleet with courage grim
  Steams forth the Tennessee.
We hem her in with battle fire—
  How furious grows the fray,
Until Surrender's flag she flies
  Above red Mobile Bay.

We count our dead, we count our scars,
  The proudest ever won;
We cheer the flag that gayly flies
  Victorious in the sun.
No longer in the rigging stands
  The hero of the day.
For he has linked his name fore'er
  To deathless Mobile Bay.

Thus I would weave a wreath for all
  Who fought with us that time,
And I'd embalm that glorious day
  For evermore in rhyme.

The stars above will rise and set,
  The years will pass away.
But brighter all the time shall grow
  The fame of Mobile Bay.

He sleeps, the bluff old Commodore
  Who led with hearty will;
But ah, methinks I see him now,
  Lashed to the rigging still.
I know that just beyond the tide,
  In God's own glorious day,
He waits to greet the gallant tars
  Who fought in Mobile Bay.

DAVID GLASCOE FARRAGUT
(*Tennessee*)

HOW THE CUMBERLAND WENT DOWN

Gray swept the angry waves
  O'er the gallant and the true,
Rolled high in mounded graves
  O'er the stately frigate's crew—
  Over cannon, over deck,
  Over all that ghastly wreck—
When the Cumberland went down.

Such a roar the waters rent
  As though a giant died,
When the wailing billows went
  Above those heroes tried;
And the sheeted foam leaped high
Like white ghosts against the sky—
  As the Cumberland went down.

O shrieking waves that gushed
  Above that loyal band,
Your cold, cold burial rushed

O'er many a heart on land,
And from all the startled North
A cry of pain broke forth,
When the Cumberland went down.

And forest old, that gave
A thousand years of power
To her lordship of the wave
And her beauty's regal dower,
Bent, as though before a blast,
When plunged her pennoned mast,
And the Cumberland went down.

And grimy mines that sent
To her their virgin strength,
And iron vigor lent
To knit her lordly length
Wildly stirred with throbs of life,
Echoes of that fatal strife,
As the Cumberland went down.

Beneath the ocean vast,
Full many a captain bold,
By many a rotting mast,
And admiral of old,
Rolled restless in his grave
As he felt the sobbing wave,
When the Cumberland went down

And stern Vikings that lay
A thousand years at rest,
In many a deep blue bay
Beneath the Baltic's breast,
Leaped on the silver sands
And shook their rusty brands;
As the Cumberland went down.

S. Weir Mitchell
(*Pennsylvania*)

A PRAYER FOR PEACE

Peace! Peace! God of our fathers grant us Peace!
Unto our cry of anguish and despair
Give ear and pity! From the lonely homes,
Where widowed beggary and orphaned woe
Fill their poor urns with tears; from trampled plains,
Where the bright harvest Thou hast sent us rots—
The blood of them who should have garnered it
Calling to Thee—from fields of carnage, where
The foul-beaked vultures, sated, flap their wings
O'er crowded corpses, that but yesterday
Bore hearts of brother, beating high with love
And common hopes and pride, all blasted now—
Father of Mercies! not alone from these
Our prayer and wail are lifted. Not alone
Upon the battle's seared and desolate track!
Nor with the sword and flame, is it, O God,
That thou hast smitten us. Around our hearths,
And in the crowded streets and busy marts,
Where echo whispers not the far-off strife
That slays our loved ones; in the solemn halls
Of safe and quiet counsel—nay, beneath
The temple roofs that we have reared to Thee,
And 'mid their rising incense—God of Peace!

The curse of war is on us. Greed and hate
Hungering for gold and blood; Ambition, bred
Of passionate vanity and sordid lusts,
Mad with the base desire of tyrannous sway
Over men's souls and thoughts, have set their price
On human hecatombs, and sell and buy
Their sons and brothers for the shambles. Priests,
With white, anointed, supplicating hands,
From Sabbath unto Sabbath clasped to Thee,
Burn in their tingling pulses, to fling down
Thy censers and Thy cross, to clutch the throats
Of kinsmen, by whose cradles they were born,

Or grasp the hand of Herod, and go forth
Till Rachel hath no children left to slay.
The very name of Jesus, writ upon
Thy shrines beneath the spotless, outstretched wings
Of Thine Almighty Dove, is wrapt and hid
With bloody battle-flags, and from the spires
That rise above them angry banners flout
The skies to which they point, amid the clang
Of rolling war-songs tuned to mock Thy praise.

All things once prized and honored are forgot;
The freedom that we worshipped next to Thee;
The manhood that was freedom's spear and shield;
The proud, true heart; the brave, outspoken word,
Which might be stifled, but could never wear
The guise, whate'er the profit, of a lie;
All these are gone, and in their stead have come
The vices of the miser and the slave—
Scorning no shame that bringeth gold or power,
Knowing no love, or faith, or reverence,
Or sympathy, or tie, or aim, or hope,
Save as begun in self, and ending there.
With vipers like to these, oh! blessed God!
Scourge us no longer! Send us down, once more,
Some shining seraph in Thy glory clad,
To wake the midnight of our sorrowing
With tidings of good-will and peace to men;
And if that star, that through the darkness led
Earth's wisdom the guide, not our folly now,
Oh, be the lightning Thine Evangelist,
With all its fiery, forked tongues, to speak
The unanswerable message of Thy will.

Peace! Peace! God of our fathers, grant us peace!
Peace to our hearts, and at Thine altars; peace
On the red waters and their blighted shores;

Peace for the 'leaguered cities, and the hosts
That watch and bleed around them and within,
Peace for the homeless and the fatherless;
Peace for the captive on his weary way,
And the mad crowds who jeer his helplessness;
For them that suffer, them that do the wrong
Sinning and sinned against. O God! for all;
For a distracted, torn, and bleeding land—
Speed the glad tidings! Give us, give us Peace!

S. Teackle Wallis

THE LEGION OF HONOR

Why are we forever speaking
  Of the warriors of old?
Men are fighting all around us,
  Full as noble, full as bold.

Ever working, ever striving,
  Mind and muscle, heart and soul,
With the reins of judgment keeping
  Passions under full control.

Noble hearts are beating boldly
  As they ever did on earth;
Swordless heroes are around us,
  Striving ever from their birth

Tearing down the old abuses,
  Building up the purer laws,
Scattering the dust of ages,
  Searching out the hidden flaws.

Acknowledging no "right divine"
  In kings and princes from the rest;
In their creed he is the noblest
  Who has worked and striven best.

Decorations do not tempt them—
  Diamond stars they laugh to scorn—
Each will wear a "Cross of Honor"
  On the Resurrection morn.

Warriors they in fields of wisdom—
  Like the noble Hebrew youth,
Striking down Goliath's error,
  With the God-blessed stone of truth.

Marshalled 'neath the Right's broad banner,
  Forward rush these volunteers,
Beating olden wrong away
  From the fast advancing years.

Contemporaries do not see them
  But the coming times will say
(Speaking of the slandered present),
  "There were heroes in that day."

Why are we then idly lying
  On the roses of our life,
While the noble-hearted struggle
  In the world-redeeming strife.

Let us rise and join the legion,
  Ever foremost in the fray—
Battling in the name of Progress
  For the nobler, purer day.

H. L. Flash

THE SOUTHERN HOMES IN RUIN

Many a gray-haired sire has died,
  As falls the oak, to rise no more,
Because his son, his prop, his pride,
  Breathed out his last all red with gore.
No more on earth, at morn, at eve,
  Shall age and youth, entwined as one—
Nor father, son, for either grieve—
  Life's work, alas, for both is done!

Many a mother's heart has bled
  While gazing on her darling child,
    As in its tiny eyes she read
  The father's image, kind and mild;
For ne'er again his voice will cheer
  The widowed heart, which mourns him dead;
Nor kisses dry the scalding tear,
  Fast falling on the orphan's head!

Many a little form will stray
  Adown the glen and o'er the hill,
And watch, with wistful looks, the way
  For him whose step is missing still;
And when the twilight steals apace
  O'er mead, and brook, and lonely home,
And shadows cloud the dear, sweet face—
  The cry will be, "Oh, papa, come!"

And many a home's in ashes now,
  Where joy was once a constant guest,
And mournful groups there are, I trow,
  With neither house nor place of rest;
And blood is on the broken sill,
  Where happy feet went to and fro,
And everywhere, by field and hill,
  Are sickening sights and sounds of woe!

There is a God who rules on high,
The widow's and the orphan's friend,
Who sees each tear and hears each sigh,
That these lone hearts to Him may send!
And when in wrath He tears away
The reasons vain which men indite,
The record book will plainest say
Who's in the wrong, and who is right.

R. B. VANCE
(*North Carolina*)

THE REAR GUARD

The guns are hushed. On every field once flowing
With war's red flood May's breath of peace is shed,
And, spring's young grass and gracious flowers are growing
Above the dead.

Ye gray old men whom we this day are greeting,
Honor to you, honor and love and trust!
Brave to the brave. Your soldier hands are meeting
Across their dust.

Bravely they fought who charged when flags were flying
In cannon's crash, in screech and scream of shell:
Bravely they fell, who lay alone and dying
In battle's hell.

Honor to them! Far graves today are flinging
Up through the soil peace-blooms to meet the sun,
And daisied heads to summer winds are singing
Their long "well done."

Our vanguard, they. They went with hot blood flushing
At battle's din, at joy of bugle's call.
They fell with smiles, the flood of young life gushing.
Full brave the fall!

But braver ye who, when the war was ended,
  And bugle's call and wave of flag were done,
Could come back home, so long left undefended.
        Your cause unwon.

And twist the useless sword to hook of reaping,
  Rebuild the homes, set back the empty chair,
And brave a land where waste and want were keeping
        Guard everywhere.

All this you did, your courage strong upon you,
  And out of ashes, wreck, a new land rose,
Through years of war no braver battle won you,
        'Gainst fiercer foes.

And now today a prospered land is cheering
  And lifting up her voice in lusty pride
For you gray men, who fought and wrought not fearing
        Battle's red tide.

Our rear guard, ye whose step is slowing, slowing,
  Whose ranks, earth-thinned, are filling other-where,
Who wore the gray—the gray, alas! still showing
        On bleaching hair.

For forty years you've watched this land grow stronger,
  For forty years you've been its bulwark, stay;
Tarry awhile; pause yet a little longer
        Upon the way.

And set our feet where there may be no turning.
  And set our faces straight on duty's track,
Where there may be for stray, strange goods no yearning
        Nor looking back.

And when for you the last tattoo has sounded,
  And on death's silent field you've pitched your tent,
When, bowed through tears, the arc of life has rounded
    To full content,

We that are left will count it guerdon royal,
  Our heritage no years can take away,
That we were born of those, unflinching, loyal,
    Who wore the gray.

IRENE FOWLER BROWN

YOUR LETTER, LADY, CAME TOO LATE

Your letter, lady, came too late,
  For Heaven had claimed its own.
Ah, sudden change—from prison rats
  Unto the great white throne!
And yet I think he would have stayed
  To live for his disdain,
Could he have read the careless words
  Which you have sent in vain.

So full of patience did he wait
  Through many a weary hour,
That o'er his simple soldier faith
  Not even death had power.
  And you—did others whisper low
  Their homage in your ear,
As though among their shadowy throng
  His spirit had a peer.

I would that you were by me now,
  To draw the sheet aside,
And see how pure the look he wore
  The moment when he died.

The sorrow that you gave him
  Had left its weary trace,
As 'twere the shadow of the cross
  Upon his pallid face.

"Her love," he said, "could change for me
  The winter's cold to spring."
Ah, trust of fickle maiden's love,
  Thou art a bitter thing!
For when these valleys bright in May
  Once more with blossoms wave,
The northern violets shall blow
  Above his humble grave.

Your dole of scanty words had been
  But one more pang to bear,
For him who kissed unto the last
  Your tress of golden hair.
I did not put it where he said,
  For when the angels come
I would not have them find the sign
  Of falsehood in the tomb.

I've seen your letter and I know
  The wiles that you have wrought
To win that noble heart of his,
  And gained it—cruel thought!
What lavish wealth men sometimes give
  For what is worthless all:
What manly bosoms beat for them
  In folly's falsest thrall.

You shall not pity him, for now
  His sorrow has an end,
Yet would that you could stand with me
  Beside my fallen friend.

And I forgive you for his sake
  As he—if it be given—
May even be pleading grace for you
  Before the court of Heaven.

Tonight the cold wind whistles by
  As I, my vigil keep
Within the prison dead house, where
  Few mourners come to weep.
A rude plank coffin holds his form,
  Yet death exalts his face
And I would rather see him thus
  Than clasped in your embrace.

Tonight your home may shine with lights
  And ring with merry song,
And you be smiling as your soul
  Had done no deadly wrong.
Your hand so fair that none would think
  It penned these words of pain;
Your skin so white—would God, your heart
  Were half as free from stain.

I'd rather be my comrade dead,
  Than you in life supreme:
For yours the sinner's waking dread,
  And his the martyr's dream.
Whom serve we in this life we serve
  In that which is to come:
He chose his way, you yours; let God
  Pronounce the fitting doom.

Col. W. S. Hawkins
(*New York*)

THE ROVING REBEL

I left my home in Virginia
  In eighteen sixty-three
I went to Pennsylvania
  A little sport to see
It's there I did get wounded
  As you can plainly see
I went to New York City,
  With a bandage on my knee.

There I boarded a steamer
  And rode some forty miles,
A way down on the seacoast,
  And to this lonesome Isle
It is a lonesome Island
  Away from Dixie's land
I wish I could get back again
  And join our Southern band.

The Yanks can never whip us,
  And that they know full well,
While Lee commands our army,
  And fame our colors swell.
We'll have our Independence,
  The Yanks will shortly see
That Dixie, oh, sweet Dixie,
  My home shall ever be.

It is a land of cotton
  Where milk and honey flows
The prettiest girls in the world
  In old Virginia grows.
I love them I adore them
  And to them I'll be true,
I'll hasten back to Dixie
  If I can just get through.

I know that old Virginia
Is the richest spot on earth
Let me hasten back to Dixie
The land of my birth.

D. F. LEMARR

While a prisoner on David's Island, N. Y., August, 1863

BROTHER, TELL ME OF THE BATTLE

Brother, tell me of the battle,
How the soldiers fought and fell;
Tell me of the weary marches,
She who loves will listen well.

Brother, draw thee close beside me,
Lay your head upon my breast,
While you're telling of the battle,
Let your fevered forehead rest.

Brother, tell me of the battle,
For they said your life was o'er;
They all told me you had fallen,
That I'd never see you more.

Oh, I've been so sad and lonely,
Filled my breast has been with pain,
Since they said my dearest brother
I should never see again.

Brother, tell me of the battle,
I can bear to hear it now;
Lay your head upon my bosom,
Let me soothe your fevered brow.

Tell me, are you badly wounded?
Did we win the deadly fight?
Did the vict'ry crown our banner?
Did you put the foe to flight?

GEORGE F. ROOT

STONEWALL'S REQUIEM

The muffled drum is beating,
  There's a sad and solemn tread,
Our Banner's draped in mourning,
  As it shrouds "th' illustrious dead."

Proud forms are bent with sorrow,
  And all Southern hearts are sore,
The Hero now is sleeping,
  Noble Stonewall is no more.

Mid the rattling of the muskets
  And the cannon's thundrous roar,
He stained the field of glory
  With his brave life's precious gore.

And though our flag waved proudly,
  We were victors ere sunset,
The gallant deeds of Chancellorsville
  Will mingle with regret.

They've borne him to an honor'd grave,
  The laurel crowns his brow,
By hallow'd James's silent wave
  He's sweetly sleeping now;

Virginia to the South is dear,
  She holds a sacred trust,
Our fallen braves from far and near
  Are covered with her dust;

She shrines the spot where now is laid
  The bravest of them all,
The martyr of our country's cause,
  Our idolized Stonewall;

But though his spirit's wafted
To the happy realms above,
His name shall live forever link'd
With reverence and love.

M. Deeves

BONNY ELOISE

The Belle of the Mohawk Vale

A song taken up by Military Bands, North and South, 1861

O, sweet is the Vale where the Mohawk gently glides
On its clear winding way to the sea,
And dearer than all storied streams on earth besides,
In this bright rolling river to me.

O, sweet are the scenes of my boyhood's sunny years,
That be-spangle the gay valley o'er,
And dear are the friends seen thro' memories' fond tears
That have lived in the blest days of yore;

O, sweet are the moments when dreaming I roam,
Thro' my loved haunts now mossy and grey,
And dear are the friends seen thro' childhood's hallow'd home,
That is crumbling now slowly away;

But sweeter dearer, yes, dearer far than these
Who charms where others all fail
Is blue-eyed, bonny, Bonny Eloise,
The Belle of the Mohawk Vale.

J. R. Thomas

THE FADED COAT OF BLUE

My brave lad sleeps in his faded coat of blue;
In a lonely grave unknown lies the heart that beat so true,
He sank faint and hungry among the famish'd brave,
And they laid him sad and lonely within his nameless grave.

He cried, "Give me water and just a little crumb,
  And my mother she will bless you thro' all the years to come;
Oh! tell my sweet sister, so gentle, good and true,
  That I'll meet her up in heaven, in my faded coat of blue."

Long, long years have vanished, and though he comes no more,
  Yet my heart will startling beat with each footfall at my door;
I gaze o'er the hill where he waved a last adieu,
  But no gallant lad I see, in his faded coat of blue.

No more the bugle calls the weary one,
  Rest, noble spirit, in the grave unknown!
I'll find you, and know you, among the good and true,
  When a robe of white is giv'n for the faded coat of blue.

J. H. McNaughton

THE VACANT CHAIR

We shall meet, but we shall miss him,
  There will be one vacant chair;
We shall linger to caress him,
  While we breathe our evening pray'r.

When a year ago we gathered,
  Joy was in his mild blue eye,
But a golden cord is severed
  And our hopes in ruin lie.

At our fireside, sad and lonely,
  Often will the bosom swell
At the remembrance of the story,
  How our noble Willie fell;

How he strove to bear our banner
  Thro' the thickest of the fight,
And uphold our country's honor,
  In the strength of manhood's might.

True, they tell us wreaths of glory
Evermore will deck his brow,
But this soothes the anguish only
Sweeping o'er our heart-strings now.

Sleep today, O early fallen,
In thy green and narrow bed,
Dirges from the pine and cypress
Mingle with the tears we shed.

We shall meet, but we shall miss him,
There will be one vacant chair;
We shall linger to caress him,
While we breathe our evening pray'r.

George F. Root

THE CONFEDERATE NOTE

Representing nothing on God's earth now,
And naught in the water below it—
As a pledge of the nation that's dead and gone,
Keep it, dear friend, and show it.

Show it to those who will lend an ear
To the tale that this paper can tell,
Of liberty born, of patriot's dream—
Of the storm cradled nation that fell.

Too poor to possess the precious ores,
And too much of a stranger to borrow,
We issued today our promise to pay,
And hope to redeem on the morrow.

The days rolled on and weeks became years,
  But our coffers were empty still,
Coin was so rare that the Treasury quaked,
  If a dollar should drop in the till.

But the faith that was in us was strong indeed,
  And our poverty well discerned;
And these little checks represented the pay,
  That our volunteers earned.

We know it had hardly value in gold,
  Yet as gold her soldier received it.
It gazed in our eyes with a promise to pay,
  And each patriot soldier believed it.

But our boys thought little of price of pay,
  Or of bills that were ever due;
We knew if it brought us bread today,
  'Twas the best our poor country could do.

Keep it, for it tells our history o'er,
  From the birth of its dreams to the last,
Modest and born of the angel Hope,
  Like the hope of success it passed.

MAJOR S. A. JONAS
(*Mississippi*)

THE LINES AROUND PETERSBURG

Oh, silence, silence! now, when night is near,
  And I am left alone,
Thou art so strange, so sad reposing here—
  And all so changed hath grown,
Where all was once exuberant with life
Through day and night, in deep and deadly strife.

If I must weep, oh, tell me, is there not
Some plaintive story breathed into mine ear
By spirit-whispers from the voiceless sphere,
  Haunting this awful spot?
To my sad soul, more mutely eloquent
Than words of fame on sculptured monument
Outspeaks yon crumbling parapet, where lies
The broken gun, the idly rusting ball,
Mute tokens of an ill-starred enterprise!
Rude altars reared for costly sacrifice!
Vast work of hero-hands left in thy fall!

Where are they now, that fearless brotherhood,
  Who marshalled here,
  That fearful year,
In pain and peril, yet undaunted stood,—
Though Death rode fiercest on the battle-storm
And earth lay strewn with many a glorious form?
Where are they now, who, when the strife was done,
With kindly greeting 'round the camp-fire met,—
And made an hour of mirth, from triumphs won,
Repay the day's stern toil, where the slow sun had set?

Where are they?—
Let the nameless grave declare,—
In strange unwonted hillocks—frequent seen!
Alas! who knows how much lies buried there!—
What worlds of love, and all that might have been!

The rest are scattered now; we know not where;
And Life to each a new employment brings;
But still they seem to gather round me here,
To whom these places were familiar things!
Wide sundered now, by mountain and by stream,
Once brothers—still a brotherhood they seem;—
More firm united, since a common woe
Hath brought to common hopes their overthrow!

Brave souls and true;—in toil and danger tried,—
I see them still as in those glorious years,
When strong, and battling bravely side by side,
All crowned their deeds with praise,—and some with tears!
'Tis done! the sword is sheathed; the banner furled,
No sound where late the crashing missile whirled—
The dead alone possess the battle-plain;
The living turn them to life's cares again.

Oh, Silence! blessed dreams upon thee wait;
Here Thought and Feeling ope their precious store,
And Memory, gathering from the spoils of Fate
Love's scattered treasures, brings them back once more!
So let me often dream,
As up the bright'ning stream
Of olden Time, thought gently leads me on,
Seeking those better days, lost, lost, alas! and gone!

SAMUEL DAVIS
(*North Carolina*)

THE OLD SERGEANT

The carrier cannot sing today the ballads
With which he used to go
Rhyming the glad rounds of the happy New Years
That are now beneath the snow.

For the same awful and portentous shadow
That overcast the earth,
And smote the land last year with desolation,
Still darkens every hearth.

And the carrier hears Beethoven's mighty death-march
Come up from every mart;
And he hears and feels it breathing in his bosom,
And beating in his heart.

And today, a scarred and weather-beaten veteran,
  Again he comes along,
To tell the story of the Old Year's struggles
  In another New Year's song.

And the song is his, but not so with the story,
  For the story, you must know,
Was told in prose to Assistant Surgeon Austin,
  By a soldier of Shiloh,—

By Robert Burton, who was brought up on the "Adams,"
  With his death-wound in his side;
And who told the story to the assistant surgeon
  On the same night that he died.

But the singer feels it will better suit the ballad,
  If all should deem it right,
To tell the story as if what it speaks of
  Had happened but last night.

"Come a little nearer, doctor,—thank you,—let me take the cup;
Draw your chair up,—draw it closer,—just another little sup!
Maybe you may think I'm better; but I'm pretty well used up,—
Doctor, you've done all you could do, but I'm just a going up!

"Feel my pulse, sir, if you want to, but it ain't much use to try—"
"Never say that," said the surgeon, as he smothered down a sigh;
"It will never do, old comrade, for a soldier to say die!"
"What you say will make no difference, doctor, when you come
  to die."

"Doctor, what has been the matter?" "You were very faint, they
  say;
You must try to get some sleep now." "Doctor, have I been
  away?"
"Not that anybody knows of!" "Doctor,—doctor, please to stay!
There is something I must tell you, and you won't have long to stay!

"I have got my marching orders, and I'm ready now to go;
Doctor, did you say I fainted?—but it couldn't ha' been so,—
For as sure as I'm a sergeant, and was wounded at Shiloh,
I've this very night been back there, on the old field of Shiloh!

"This is all that I remember! The last time the lighter came,
And the lights had all been lowered, and the noises much the same,
He had not been gone five minutes before something called my
name:
'Orderly Sergeant—Robert Burton!' just that way it called my
name,

"And I wondered who could call me so distinctly and so slow,
Knew it couldn't be the lighter, he could not have spoken so,
And I tried to answer, 'Here, sir!' but I couldn't make it go!
For I couldn't move a muscle, and I couldn't make it go!

"Then I thought: 'It's all a nightmare, all a humbug and a bore;
Just another foolish grape-vine,—and it won't come any more;'
But it came, sir, notwithstanding, just the same way as before:
'Orderly Sergeant—Robert Burton!' even plainer than before.

"That is all that I remember, till a sudden burst of light,
And I stood beside the river, where we stood that Sunday night,
Waiting to be ferried over to the dark bluffs opposite,
When the river was perdition and all hell was opposite!

"And the same old palpitation came again in all its power,
And I heard a bugle sounding, as from some celestial tower;
And the same mysterious voice said: 'It is the eleventh hour!
Orderly Sergeant—Robert Burton,—It is the eleventh hour!'

"Doctor Austin! What day is this?" "It is Wednesday night,
you know."
"Yes,—tomorrow will be New Year's, and a right good time below!
What time is it, Doctor Austin?" "Nearly twelve." "Then don't
you go!
Can it be that all this happened—all this—not an hour ago?

"There was where the gunboats opened on the dark rebellious host;
And where Webster semicircled his last guns upon the coast;
There were still the two log-houses, just the same, or else their ghost!
And the same old transport came and took me over,—or its ghost!

"And the old field lay before me all deserted far and wide;
There was where they fell on Prentiss,—there McClernand met the tide;
There was where stern Sherman rallied, and where Hurlbut's heroes died,—
Lower down where Wallace charged them, and kept charging till he died.

"There was where Lew Wallace showed them he was of the canny kin;
There was where old Nelson thundered, and where Rousseau waded in;
There McCook sent 'em to breakfast, and we all began to win;—
There was where the grape-shot took me, just as we began to win.

"Now a shroud of snow and silence over everything was spread;
And but for this old blue mantle and the old hat on my head,
I should not have even doubted, to this moment, I was dead!
For my footsteps were as silent as the snow upon the dead!

"Death and silence!—death and silence! all around me as I sped!
And behold a mighty tower, as if builded to the dead,
To the heaven of the heavens, lifted up its mighty head,
Till the stars and stripes of heaven all seemed waving from its head!

"Round and mighty-based it towered,—up into the infinite,—
And I knew no mortal mason could have built a shaft so bright;
For it shone like solid sunshine; and a winding stair of light
Wound around it and around it till it wound clear out of sight!

"And, behold, as I approached it, with a rapt and dazzled stare,—
Thinking that I saw old comrades just ascending the great stair,—
Suddenly the solemn challenge broke off—'Halt, and who goes there?'
'I'm a friend,' I said, 'If you are.' 'Then advance, sir, to the stair!'

"I advanced!—That sentry, doctor, was Elijah Ballantyne!—
First of all to fall on Monday, after we had formed the line!—
'Welcome, my old sergeant, welcome! Welcome by that countersign!'
And he pointed to the scar there, under this old cloak of mine!

"As he grasped my hand, I shuddered, thinking only of the grave;
But he smiled and pointed upward with a bright and bloodless glaive;
'That's the way, sir, to head-quarters!' 'What head-quarters?' 'Of the brave!'
'But the great tower?' 'That', he answered, 'is the way, sir, of the brave!'

"Then a sudden shame came o'er me at his uniform of light;
At my own so old and tattered, and at his so new and bright.
'Ah!' said he, 'you have forgotten the new uniform tonight,—
Hurry back, for you must be here at just twelve o'clock to-night!

"And the next thing I remember, you were sitting *there*, and I—
Doctor,—did you hear a footstep? Hark!—God bless you all! Good-by!
Doctor, please to give my musket and my knapsack, when I die,
To my son—my son that's coming—he won't get here till I die!

"Tell him his old father blessed him as he never did before,—
And to carry that old musket—" Hark! a knock is at the door—
"Tell the Union—" See! it opens!—"Father! Father! speak once more!"
"Bless you!" gasped the old gray sergeant,—and he lay and said no more!

FORCEYTHE WILLSON
(*Indiana*)

THE SOUTHERN DEAD

Where are the men who at the call
  Of duty battled for the right,
Who to their country gave their all
  And bore our banner in the fight?
Ye winged winds that round them play,
  Where are these noble men today?

"Each one a soldier's coffin fills,"
  The answer comes in plaintive moan;
"They rest upon a hundred hills
  Unmarked, unhonored and unknown,"
Or else their bones uncoffined lie
  Beneath Virginia's weeping sky.

The flower of old Virginia's pride
  With bounding heart sped to the foe,
And grappling bravely hand to hand,
  For Southern honor struck the blow,
Resolved to free their homes opprest
  Or on their broken shields to rest.

And there they fell, perchance 'twas meet
  (They knew not then their country's fall),
The stars and bars their winding sheet,
  The blood-laved earth their funeral pall,
While trysting nature o'er their graves
In vernal beauty blooms and waves.

And shall they unremembered lie
  Save by the flowers and grasses wild?
What says the State? Does she reply,
  I care not for my soldier child?
Avaunt the thought! Oh, mother, turn,
And deck the son's neglected urn.

Who doubts that had our guardian star
  Rained fortune on our struggling band,
The bright memorials of the war
  Had crowned each hill-top in the land,
And angels waked from Parian bed
Their white wings o'er the sleepers spread?

Oh, who can paint the pageant bright
  When (five-and twenty years sped by)
Thou pressed again the historic site
On yonder Capitolian height,
  Where Dixie's flag first leap'd on high,
  Amid the new-born nation's cry!

Sun never graced a scene more grand!
  Nor wilder shouts could mortals raise,
When Pettus stood with veteran band
And scar-marked Gordon took the stand,
  Flashing the light of other days,—
  Speaking the Southern leader's praise!

And thus t'will be till time shall end,—
  The world shall with thy plaudits ring,
Great hist'ry shall thy name defend,
Sculpture its guardian graces lend,
  And future bards shall joy to sing
  The glories of our uncrowned king.

"Peace hath its victories great as war,"
  Oh, bright example here we find!
While England boasts her Trafalgar,
We point with pleasure to Beauvoir,
  Where stainless Honor sits enshrined
Within a true and constant mind.

Enjoy then, sire, thy cherished rest
  From care and strife and sorrow free;
And when thy sun shall seek the west,
Thy Mother take thee to her breast,
  The music of the sounding sea
  Shall thy perpetual requiem be!

Till then, bloom on, ye roses sweet,
  Ye forests waft your fragrant gales,
Sweet birds your loveliest lays repeat.
  Join in, O sea, with chorus meet,—
Oh, Thou, whose mercy never fails,
  Spare him who treads these smiling vales!

Yet not in old Westminster's aisle,
  Where sculptured glory lifts its charms,
Can there be viewed a holier pile
  Than that we build to Southern arms?
Could heroes serve a cause more just,
Or crypts enshrine more sacred dust?

We've waited long the shaft to rear,
  'Tis well our braves unconscious sleep,
Or eyes that cannot know a tear
  O'er man's ingratitude would weep.
Ah! but for woman, brave and pure,
How long would Southern fame endure?

Then let our column pierce the sky,
  Rise tall and graceful from the square,
And then should glorious Freedom die,
  Her spirit still may linger there,
And sweet communion hold with those
Who never quailed before their foes.

MORTON BRYAN WHARTON, D. D.

THE LAST CHARGE AT APPOMATTOX

Scarred on a hundred fields before,
Naked and starved and travel-sore,
  Each man a tiger hunted,
They stood at bay as brave as Huns—
Last of the Old South's splendid sons,
Flanked by ten thousand shotted guns,
  And by ten thousand fronted.

Scorched by the cannon's molten breath,
They'd climbed the trembling walls of death
  And set their standards tattered—
Had charged at the bugle's stirring blare
Through bolted gloom and godless glare
From the dead's reddened gulches, where
  The searching shrapnel shattered.

They formed—that Carolina band—
With Grimes, the Spartan, in command,
  And, at the word of Gordan,
Through splintered fire and stifling smoke—
They struck with lightning's scathing stroke,—
Those doomed and desperate men—and broke
  Across the iron cordon.

They turned in sullen, slow retreat—
Ah, there are laurels of defeat—
  Turned, for the chief had spoken;
With one last shot hurled back the foe,
And prayed the trump of doom to blow,
Now that the Southern stars were low
  The Southern bars were broken.

Some time the calm, impartial years
Will tell what made them dead to tears
  Of loved ones left to languish:—

What nerved them for the lonely guard,
For cleaving blade and mangling shard,—
What gave them strength in tent and ward
  To drain the dregs of anguish.

But the far ages will propound
What never sage hath lore to sound;—
  Why, in such fires of rancor,
The God of love should find it meet
For Him, with Grant as sledge to beat
On Lee, the anvil, at such heat,
  Our nation's great sheet-anchor.

HENRY JEROME STOCKARD
(*North Carolina*)

THE PHANTOM HOST

My form was wrapped in the slumber
  Which steals from the heart its cares,
For my life was weary
  With its barren waste of years;
But my soul, with rapid pinions,
  Fled swift to the light which seems
From a phantom's sun and planets
  For the dreamer in his dreams.

I stood in a wondrous woodland,
  Where the sunlight nestled sweet
In the cups of snowy lilies
  Which grew about my feet;
And while the Gothic forest arches
  Stirred gently with the air
The lilies underneath them
  Swung their censers pale in prayer.

I stood amazed and wondering,
  And a grand memoriam strain
Came sweeping through the forest,
  And died; then rose again.
It swelled in solemn measure,
  Till my soul, with comfort blessed,
Sank down among the lilies
  With folded wings to rest.

Then to that mystic music
  Through the forest's twilight aisle
Passed a host with muffled footsteps
  In martial rank and file;
And I knew those gray-clad figures,
  Thus slowly passing by,
Were the souls of Southern soldiers
  Who for freedom dared to die.

In front rode Sidney Johnston,
  With a brow no longer wrung
By the vile and senseless slanders
Of a prurient rabble tongue;
  And near him mighty Jackson,
With a placid front, as one
Whose warfare was accomplished,
  Whose crown of glory won.

There Hill, too, pure and noble,
  Passed in the spirit train,
For he joined the martyred army
  From the South's last battle plain.
The next in order followed
  The warrior-priest, great Polk,
With joy to meet his Master,
  For he had nobly borne the yoke.

There Stuart, the bold, the daring;
  With matchless Pelham rode;
With earnest, chastened faces,
  They were looking up to God.
And Jenkins, glorious Jenkins,
  With his patient, fearless eyes,
And the brave devoted Garnett,
  Journeyed on to Paradise.

Before a shadowy squadron
  Rode Morgan, keen and strong,
And I knew by his tranquil forehead
  He'd forgotten every wrong.
There peerless Pegram marching
  With a dauntless, martial tread,
And I breathed a sigh for the hero,
  The young, the early dead.

'Mid spectral black-horse troopers
  Passed Ashby's stalwart form,
With that proud, defiant bearing
  Which so spurned the battle storm;
But his glance was mild and tender,
  For in that Phantom Host
He dwelt with lingering fondness
  On the brother he had lost.

Then strode the brave Maloney,
  Kind, genial adjutant;
And next him walked the truthful,
  The lion-hearted Gantt.
There to that solemn music
  Passed a triad of the brave:
Lomax, Phelan, Alfred Pinckney—
  All had found a soldier's grave.

They were young and gentle spirits,
  But they quaffed the bitter cup,
For their country's flag was falling,
  And they fell to lift it up.
And then passed in countless thousands
  In that mighty phantom host
True hearts and noble patriots
  Whose names on earth are lost.

There "the missing" found their places—
  Those who vanished from our gaze
Like brilliant, flashing meteors,
  And were lost in glory's blaze.
Yes, they passed, that noble army—
  They passed to meet their Lord;
And a voice within me whispered;
  "They but march to their reward."

REV. PERONNEAN D. HAY

ODE

Sleep sweetly in your humble graves,
  Sleep, martyrs of a fallen cause;
Though yet no marble column craves
  The pilgrim here to pause.

In seeds of laurel in the earth,
  The blossom of your fame is blown,
And somewhere, waiting for its birth,
  The shaft is in the stone.

Meanwhile, behalf the tardy years
  Which keep in trust your storied tombs,
Behold your sisters bring their tears,
  And these memorial blooms.

Small tributes but your shades will smile
  More proudly on these wreaths today,
Than when some cannon-moulded pile
  Shall overlook this bay.

Stoop, angels, hither from the skies,
  There is no holier spot of ground,
Than where defeated valor lies,
  By mourning beauty crowned.

HENRY TIMROD

ABRAHAM LINCOLN

Oh, slow to smite and swift to spare,
  Gentle and merciful and just,
Who, in the fear of God, didst bear
  The sword of power, a nation's trust.

In sorrow by thy bier we stand,
  Amid the awe that hushes all,
And speak the anguish of a land
  That shook with horror at thy fall.

Thy task is done; the bound are free;
  We bear thee to an honored grave,
Whose proudest monument shall be
  The broken fetters of the slave.

Pure was thy life; its bloody close
  Hath placed thee with the sons of light,
Among the noble host of those
  Who perished in the cause of Right.

WILLIAM CULLEN BRYANT
(*Massachusetts*)

ROBERT E. LEE

A gallant foeman in the fight,
  A brother when the fight was o'er,
The hand that led the host with might
  The blessed torch of learning bore.

No shriek of shells nor roll of drums,
  No challenge fierce, resounding far,
When reconciling Wisdom comes
  To heal the cruel wounds of war.

Thought may the minds of men divide,
  Love makes the heart of nations one,
And so, the soldier grave beside,
  We honor thee, Virginia's son.

JULIA WARD HOWE
(*Massachusetts*)

HIGH TIDE AT GETTYSBURG

A cloud possessed the hollow field,
The gathering battle's smoky shield;
  Athwart the gloom the lightning flashed,
  And through the cloud some horsemen dashed
And from the heights the thunder pealed.

Then, at the brief command of Lee,
Moved out the matchless infantry,
  With Pickett leading grandly down,
  To rush against the roaring crown
Of those dread heights of destiny.

Far heard above the angry guns,
A cry across the tumult runs;
  The voice that rang through Shiloh's woods.
  And Chickamauga's solitudes;
The fierce South cheering on her sons.

Ah, how the withering tempest blew
Against the front of Pettigrew;
A khamsin wind that scorched and singed,
Like that infernal flame that fringed
The British squares at Waterloo;

A thousand fell where Kemper led;
A thousand died where Garnett bled;
In blinding flame and strangling smoke,
The remnant through the batteries broke
And crossed the works with Armistead.

"Once more in Glory's van with me,"
Virginia cries to Tennessee;
"We two together, come what may,
Shall stand upon those works today"—
The reddest day in history.

Brave Tennessee, reckless the way,
Virginia heard her comrade say;
"Close round this rent and riddled rag"
What time she set her battle-flag
Amid the guns of Doubleday.

But who shall break the guards that wait
Before the awful face of fate?
The tattered standards of the South
Were shrivelled at the cannon's mouth,
And all her hopes were desolate.

In vain the Tennessean set
His breast against the bayonet;
In vain Virginia charged and raged,
A tigress in her wrath uncaged,
Till all the hill was red and wet.

Above the bayonets mixed and crossed
Men saw a gray, gigantic ghost
  Receding through the battle cloud,
  And heard across the tempest loud
The death-cry of a nation lost.

The brave went down, without disgrace
They leaped to ruin's red embrace;
  They only heard fame's thunder wake,
  And saw the dazzling sunburst break
In smiles on glory's bloody face,

They fell who lifted up a hand,
And bade the sun in heaven to stand;
  They smote and fell who set the bars
  Against the progress of the stars,
And stayed the march of Motherland.

They stood who saw the future come
On through the fight's delirium;
  They smote and stood who held the hope
  Of nations on that slippery slope,
Amid the cheers of Christendom.

God lives, He forged the iron will,
That clutched and held that trembling hill,
  God lives and reigns, He built and lent
  The heights for Freedom's battlement,
Where floats her flag in triumph still.

Fold up the banners, smelt the guns,
Love rules. Her gentle purpose runs
  A mighty mother turns in tears
  The pages of her battle years.
Lamenting all her fallen sons.

WILL H. THOMPSON
(*Indiana*)

THE FIGHT AT FORT SUMTER

'Twas a wonderful brave fight,
Through the day and all night,
March, Halt, Left, Right,
  So they formed;
And one thousand to ten,
The bold Palmetto men
  Sumter stormed.

The smoke in a cloud
Closed her in like a shroud,
While the cannon roared aloud
  From the port;
And the red cannon-balls
Ploughed the granite walls
  Of the Fort.

Sumter's gunners at their places,
With their gunpowdered faces,
Shook their shoulders from their braces,
  And stripped
Stark and white to the waist
Just to give the foe a taste,
  And be whipped.

In the town, through every street,
Tramp, tramp went the feet,
For they said the Federal fleet
  Hove in sight;
And down the wharves they ran,
Every woman, child, and man,
  To the fight.

On the fort the old flag waved,
And the barking batteries braved,

While the bold seven thousand raved
  As they fought;
For each blinding sheet of flame
From her cannon thundered shame,—
  So they thought.

And strange enough to tell
Though the gunners fired well,
And the balls ploughed red as hell
  Through the dirt;
Though the shells burst and scattered,
And fortress walls were shattered,—
  None was hurt.

But the fort—so hot she grew,
As the cannon-balls flew,
That each man began to stew
  At his gun;
They were not afraid to die,
But this making Patriot pie
  Was not fun.

So, to make the story short,
The traitors got the fort
After thirty hours' sport
  With the balls;
But the victory is not theirs,
Though the brazen banner flares
  From the walls.

It were better they should dare
The lion in his lair,
Or defy the grizzly bear
  In his den,
Than to wake the fearful cry
That is rising up on high
  From our men.

To our banner we are clinging,
And a song we are singing,
Whose chorus is ringing
  From each mouth,
'Tis "The Old Constitution
And a stern retribution
  To the South."

AUTHOR UNKNOWN

Vanity Fair, April 27, 1861

THE JACKET OF GRAY

Fold it up carefully, lay it aside;
Tenderly touch it, look on it with pride;
For dear to our hearts must it be evermore,
The jacket of gray our loved soldier-boy wore.

Can we ever forget when he joined the brave band
That rose in defense of our dear Southern land,
And in his bright youth hurried on to the fray,
How proudly he donned it—the jacket of gray?

His fond mother blessed him, and looked up above,
Commending to heaven the child of her love;
What anguish was hers mortal tongue can not say,
When he passed from her sight in the jacket of gray.

But her country had called and she would not repine,
Though costly the sacrifice placed on its shrine;
Her heart's dearest hopes on its altar she lay,
When she sent out her boy in the jacket of gray.

Months passed, and war's thunder rolled over the land,
Unsheathed was the sword, and lighted the brand;
We heard in the distance the sound of the fray,
And prayed for our boy in the jacket of gray.

Ah vain, all in vain, were our prayers and our tears,
The glad shout of victory rang in our ears;
But our treasured one on the red battle-field lay,
While the life-blood oozed out on the jacket of gray.

His young comrades found him, and tenderly bore
The cold lifeless form to his home by the shore;
Oh, dark were our hearts on that terrible day,
When we saw our dead boy in the jacket of gray.

Ah, spotted and tattered, and stained now with gore,
Was the garment which once he so proudly wore;
We bitterly wept as we took it away,
And replaced with death's white robe the jacket of gray.

We laid him to rest in his cold narrow bed,
And graved on the marble we placed o'er his head
As the proudest tribute our sad hearts could pay—
"He never disgraced it, the jacket of gray."

Then fold it up carefully, lay it aside,
Tenderly touch it, look on it with pride;
For dear must it be to our hearts evermore,
The jacket of gray our loved soldier-boy wore!

Caroline A. Ball

LEE AT THE WILDERNESS

'Twas a terrible moment!
  The blood and the rout!
His great bosom shook
  With an awful doubt,
Confusion in front,
  And a pause in the cries;
And a darkness like night
  Passed over our skies;
  There were tears in the eyes
    Of General Lee.

As the blue-clad lines
  Swept fearfully near,
There was waving yonder,
  And a break in the cheer
Of our columns unsteady;
  But, "We are here! We are ready
With rifle and blade,"
  Cried the Texas Brigade
    To General Lee.

He smiles—it meant death,
  That wonderful smile;
It leaped like a flame
  Down each close-set file;
And we stormed to the front
  With a long, loud cry—
We had long ago learned
  How to charge, and to die;
  There was faith in the eye
    Of General Lee.

But a sudden pause came,
  As we dashed on the foe,
And our seething columns
  Swayed to and fro:
Cold grew our blood,
  Glowing like wine,
And a quick, sharp whisper
  Shot over our line,
As our rank opened wide;
And there by one side
    Rode General Lee.

How grandly he rode!
  With his eyes on fire
As his great bosom shook

With an awful desire!
But, "Back to the rear!
Till you ride to the rear,
We will not do battle
With gun or with blade!"
Cried the Texas Brigade
To General Lee.

And so he rode back;
And our terrible yell
Stormed up to the front;
And the fierce, wild swell,
And the roar and the rattle,
Swept into the battle
From General Lee.

I felt my foot slip
In the gathering fray—
I looked, and my brother
Lay dead in my way.
I paused but one moment,
To draw him aside:
Ah, the gash in his bosom
Was bloody and wide!
But he smiled, for he died
For General Lee

Christ! 'twas maddening work;
But the work was done,
And a few came back
When the hour was won.
Let it glow in the peerless
Records of the fearless—
The charge that was made
By the Texas Brigade
For General Lee.

MOLLIE E. MOORE DAVIS
(*Texas*)

THE SOUTHERN SOLDIER BOY

Young as the youngest who donned the gray,
True as the truest who wore it,
Brave as the bravest he marched away,
(Hot tears on the cheeks of his mother lay);
Triumphant waved our flag one day,
He fell in front before it.

CHORUS

A grave in the wood with the grass o'er grown
A grave in the heart of his mother,
His clay in the one lifeless and lone,
But his memory lives in the other.

Firm as the firmest where duty led,
He hurried without a falter;
Bold as the boldest he fought and bled,
And the day was won but the field was red;
And the blood of his fresh young heart was shed,
On his country's hallowed altar.

CHORUS

On the trampled breast of the battle plain,
Where the foremost ranks had wrestled,
The fairest form 'mid all the slain
Like a child asleep he nestled.
In the solemn of the woods that swept
The field where his comrades found him,
They buried him there, and strong men wept,
As in silence they gathered 'round him.

CHORUS

FATHER RYAN
(*Virginia*)

SONG OF THE TEXAS RANGERS

The morning star is paling,
  The camp-fires flicker low;
Our steeds are madly neighing,
  For the bugle bids us go.
So put thc foot in stirrup,
  And shake the bridle free,
For today the Texas Rangers
  Must cross the Tennessee.
With Wharton for our leader,
  We'll chase the dastard foe,
Till our horses bathe their fetlocks
  In the deep blue Ohio.

Our men are from the prairies,
  That roll broad and proud and free,
From the high and craggy mountains
  To the murmuring Mexic sea;
And their hearts are open as their plains,
  Their thoughts as proudly brave
As the bold cliffs of the San Bernard,
  Or the Gulf's resistless wave.
Then quick into the saddle,
  And shake the bridle free,
Today with gallant Wharton,
  We cross the Tennessee.

'Tis joy to be a ranger!
  To fight for dear Southland;
'Tis joy to follow Wharton,
  With his gallant, trusty band!
'Tis joy to see our Harrison,
  Plunge like a meteor bright
Into the thickest of the fray,
  And deal his deathly might.

Oh! who'd not be a Ranger,
  And follow Wharton's cry!
To battle for his country—
  And, if it needs be—die!

By the Colorado's waters,
  On the Gulf's deep murmuring shore,
On our soft green peaceful prairies
  Are the homes we may see no more;
But in those homes our gentle wives,
  And mothers with silv'ry hairs,
Are loving us with tender hearts,
  And shielding us with prayers.
So, trusting in our country's God,
  We draw our stout, good brand,
For those we love at home,
  Our altars and our land.

Up, up with the crimson battle-flag—
  Let the blue pennon fly;
Our steeds are stamping proudly—
  They hear the battle-cry!
The thundering bomb, the bugle's call,
  Proclaim the foe is near;
We strike for God and native land,
  And all we hold most dear.
Then spring into the saddle,
  And shake the bridle free,
For Wharton leads, through fire and blood,
  For home and Victory!

AUTHOR UNKNOWN

TO ABRAHAM LINCOLN

(Sonnet 1862)

Stern be the pilot in the dreadful hour
When a great nation, like a ship at sea
With the wroth breakers whitening at her lee,
Feels her last shudder if her helmsman cower;
A Godlike manhood be his mighty dower,
Such and so gifted, Lincoln, mayest thou be,
With thy high wisdom's low simplicity
And awful tenderness of voted power.
From our hot records then thy name shall stand
On Time's calm ledger out of passionate days—
With the pure debt of gratitude begun,
And only paid in never-ending praise—
One of the many of a mighty Land,
Made by God's providence the Anointed One.

JOHN JAMES PIATT
(Ohio)

THE NEW DIXIE

I wish I was in the land of cotton,
Cinnamon seed and sandy bottom;
  Look away, away, away down South in Dixie.
Her scenes shall fade from my memory never;
For Dixie's land hurrah forever;
  Look away, away, away down South in Dixie.

I wish I was in Dixie;
  Away, away;
In Dixie's land I'll take my stand,
And live and die in Dixie.
  Away, away,
Away down South in Dixie.

Her lot may be hard, her skies may darken;
To Dixie's voice we'll ever hearken;
  Look away, away, away down South in Dixie.
The coward may shirk, the wretch go whining,
But we'll be true till the sun stops shining,
  Look away, away, away down South in Dixie.

By foes begirt and friends forsaken,
The faith of her sons is still unshaken;
  Look away, away, away down South in Dixie.
For Dixie's land and Dixie's nation,
We'll stand and fight the whole creation;
  Look away, away, away down South in Dixie.

The Dixie girls wear homespun cotton,
But their winning smiles I've not forgotten;
  Look away, away, away down South in Dixie.
They've won my heart and naught surpasses
My love for the bright-eyed Dixie lassies;
  Look away, away, away down South in Dixie.

Then up with the flag that leads to glory;
A thousand years 'twill live in story;
  Look away, away, away down South in Dixie.
The Southron's pride, the foeman's wonder,
The flag that the Dixie boys march under;
  Look away, away, away down South in Dixie.

I'll give my life for Dixie;
    Away, away;
In Dixie's land I'll take my stand,
And live and die in Dixie.
    Away, away,
Away down South in Dixie.

MARIA LOUISA EVE
(Georgia)

ALL QUIET ALONG THE POTOMAC TONIGHT

All quiet along the Potomac, they say,
  Except here and there a stray picket
Is shot, as he walks on his beat to and fro,
  By a rifleman hid in the thicket,
'Tis nothing, a private or two now and then,
  Will not count in the news of the battle.
Not an officer lost, only one of the men
  Moaning out all alone the death-rattle.

All quiet along the Potomac tonight,
  Where the soldiers lie peacefully dreaming;
Their tents in the rays of the clear autumn moon
  Or in the light of their camp-fires gleaming;
A tremulous sigh, as a gentle night wind,
  Through the forest leaves softly is creeping,
While the stars up above, with their glittering eyes,
  Keep guard o'er the army while sleeping.

There's only the sound of the lone sentry's tread,
  As he tramps from the rock to the fountain,
And thinks of the two on the low trundle-bed,
  Far away in the cot on the mountain.
His musket falls slack, and his face, dark and grim,
  Grows gentle with memories tender
As he mutters a prayer for the children asleep;
  For their mother,—may heaven defend her!

The moon seems to shine as brightly as then,—
  That night when the love yet unspoken
Leaped up to his sealed lips, and when low-murmured vows
  Were pledged to be ever unbroken.
Then drawing his sleeve roughly over his eyes,
  He dashes off tears that are welling,
And gathers his gun close up to its place,
  As if to keep down the heart-swelling.

He passes the fountain, the blasted pine tree;
The footsteps are lagging and weary;
Yet onward they go, through the broad belt of light,
Toward the shade of the forest so dreary.
Hark! was it the night-wind rustled the leaves?
Was it moonlight so wondrously flashing?
It looked like a rifle! "Ha! Mary, good-by."
And the life-blood is ebbing and splashing.

All quiet along the Potomac tonight,
No sound save the rush of the river;
Whilst soft falls the dew on the face of the dead,—
The picket's off duty forever!

LAMAR FONTAINE

THE PALMETTO AND THE PINE

They have planted them together—our gallant sires of old—
Though one was crowned with crystal snow, and one with solar gold.
They planted them together—on the world's majestic height;
At Saratoga's deathless charge; at Eutaw's stubborn fight;
At midnight on the dark redoubt, 'mid plunging shot and shell.
At noontide, gasping in the crush of battle's bloody swell.
With gory hands and reeking brows, amid the mighty fray
Which surged and swelled around them on that memorable day.
When they planted Independence as a symbol and a sign,
They struck deep soil, and planted the palmetto and the pine.
They planted them together,—by the river of the years—
Watered with our fathers' hearts' blood, watered with our mothers' tears;
In the strong rich soil of freedom, with a bounteous benison
From their prophet, priest, and pioneer—our father, Washington;
Above them floated echoes of the ruin and the wreck,
Like "drums that beat at Louisburg, and thundered at Quebec;"

But the old lights sank in darkness as the new stars rose to shine
O'er those emblems of the sections, the palmetto and the pine.
And we'll plant them still together—for 'tis yet the self-same soil
Our fathers' valor won for us by victory and toil;
On Florida's fair everglades, by bold Ontario's flood—
And through them send electric life, as leaps the kindred blood;
For thus it is they taught us who for freedom lived and died—
The Eternal's law of justice must and shall be justified,
That God has joined together, by a fiat all divine,
The destinies of dwellers 'neath the palm-tree and the pine.
God plant them still together. Let them flourish side by side
In the halls of our Centennial, mailed in more than marble pride;
With kindly deeds and noble names we'll grave them o'er and o'er,
With brave historic legends of glorious days of yore;
While the clear, exultant chorus, rising from united bands;
The echo of our triumph peals to earth's remotest lands;
While "faith, fraternity, and love" shall joyfully entwine
Around our chosen emblems, the palmetto and the pine.
"Together" shouts Niagara, his thunder-toned decree;
"Together" echo back the waves upon the Mexic Sea;
"Together" sing the sylvan hills where old Atlantic roars;
"Together" boom the breakers on the wild Pacific shores;
"Together" cry the people. And "together" it shall be,
An everlasting charter-bond forever for the free;
Of liberty the signet-seal, the one eternal sign,
Be those united emblems—the palmetto and the pine.

L. Virginia Smith French

ZOLLICOFFER

First in the fight, and first in the arms
Of the white-winged angels of glory,
With the heart of the South at the feet of God,
And his wounds to tell the story;

For the blood that flowed from his hero heart,
  On the spot where he nobly perished,
Was drunk by the earth as a sacrament
  In the holy cause he cherished!

In Heaven a home with the brave and blessed.
  And for his soul's sustaining
The apocalyptic eyes of Christ—
  And nothing on earth remaining,

But a handful of dust in the land of his choice,
  A name in song and story—
And fame to shout with immortal voice
  Dead on the field of Glory!

HENRY LYNDEN FLASH
(Tennessee)

GETTYSBURG

There was no union in the land,
  Though wise men labored long
With links of clay and ropes of sand
  To bind the right and wrong.

There was no temper in the blade
  That once could cleave a chain;
Its edge was dull with touch of trade
  And clogged with rust of gain.

The sand and clay must shrink away
  Before the lava tide:
By blows and blood and fire assay
  The metal must be tried.

Here sledge and anvil met, and when
  The furnace fiercest roared,
God's undiscerning workingmen
  Reforged His people's sword.

Enough for them to ask and know
  The moment's duty clear—
The bayonets flashed it there below,
  The guns proclaimed it here:

To do and dare, and die at need,
  But while life lasts, to fight—
For right or wrong a simple creed,
  But simplest for the right.

They faltered not who stood that day
  And held this post of dread;
Nor cowards they who wore the gray
  Until the gray was red.

For every wreath the victor wears
  The vanquished half may claim;
And every monument declares
  A common pride and fame.

We raise no altar stones to Hate,
  Who never bowed to Fear:
No province crouches at our gate,
  To shame our triumph here.

Here standing by a dead wrong's grave
  The blindest now may see,
The blow that liberates the slave
  But sets the master free!

When ills beset the nation's life
  Too dangerous to bear,
The sword must be the surgeon's knife,
  Too merciful to spare.

O Soldier of our common land,
'Tis thine to bear that blade
Loose in the sheath, or firm in hand,
But ever unafraid.

When foreign foes assail our right,
One nation trusts to thee—
To wield it well in worthy fight—
The sword of Meade and Lee!

JAMES JEFFREY ROCHE
(*Michigan*)

LINCOLN AT GETTYSBURG

After the eyes that looked, the lips that spoke
Here, from the shadows of impending death,
Those words of solemn breath,
What voice may fitly break
The silence, doubly hallowed, left by him?
We can but bow the head, with eyes grown dim,
And, as a Nation's litany, repeat
The phrase his martyrdom hath made complete,
Noble as then, but now more sadly sweet;
"Let us, the Living, rather dedicate
Ourselves to the unfinished work, which they
Thus far advanced so nobly on its way,
And save the perilled State!
Let us, upon this field where they, the brave,
Their last full measure of devotion gave,
Highly resolve they have not died in vain!—
That, under God, the Nation's later birth
Of Freedom, and the people's gain
Of their own Sovereignty, shall never wane
And perish from the circle of the earth!"
From such a perfect text, shall Song aspire
To light her faded fire,
And into wandering music turn

Its virtue, simple, sorrowful, and stern?
His voice all elegies anticipated;
  For, whatsoe'er the strain,
  We hear that one refrain:
"We consecrate ourselves to them, the Consecrated!"

BAYARD TAYLOR

TO MY SOLDIER BROTHER

When softly gathering shades of ev'n
  Creep o'er the prairies broad and green,
And countless stars bespangle heav'n,
  And fringe the clouds with silv'ry sheen,
My fondest sigh to thee is giv'n,
My lonely wand'ring soldier boy;
  And thoughts of thee
  Steal over me
Like ev'ning shade, my soldier boy.

My brother, though thou'rt far away,
  And dangers hurtle round thy path,
And battle lightnings o'er thee play,
  And thunders peal in awful wrath,
Think, whilst thou'rt in the hot affray,
Thy sister prays for thee, my boy.
  If fondest prayer
  Can shield thee there
Sweet angels guard my soldier boy.

Thy proud young heart is beating high
  To clash of arms and cannon's roar;
That firm-set lip and flashing eye
  Tell how thy heart is brimming o'er.
Be free and live, be free or die;
Be that thy motto now, my boy;
  And though thy name's
  Unknown to fame,
'Tis graven on my heart, my boy.

SALLIE M. BALLARD
(*Texas*)

ALBERT SIDNEY JOHNSTON

I hear again the tread of war go thundering through the land,
And Puritan and Cavalier are clinching neck and hand,
Round Shiloh church the furious foes have met to thrust and slay,
Where erst the peaceful sons of Christ were wont to kneel and pray.

The wrestling of the ages shakes the hills of Tennessee,
With all their echoing mounts a-throb with war's wild minstrelsy;
A galaxy of stars new-born round the shield of Mars,
And set against the Stars and Stripes the flashing Stars and Bars.

'Twas Albert Sidney Johnston led the columns of the Gray,
Like Hector on the plains of Troy his presence fired the fray;
And dashing horse and gleaming sword spake out his royal will
As on the slopes of Shiloh field the blasts of war blew shrill.

"Down with the base invaders," the Gray shout forth the cry,
"Death to presumptuous rebels," the Blue ring out reply;
All day the conflict rages and yet again all day,
Though Grant is on the Union side he cannot stem nor stay.

They are a royal race of men, these brothers face to face,
Their fury speaking through their guns, their frenzy in their pace;
The sweeping onset of the Gray bears down the sturdy Blue,
Though Sherman and his legions are heroes through and through.

Though Prentiss and his gallant men are forcing scaur and crag,
They fall like sheaves before the scythes of Hardee and of Bragg;
Ah, who shall tell the victor's tale when all the strife is past,
When man and man in one great mould the men who strive are cast.

As when the Trojan hero came from that fair city's gates,
With tossing mane and flaming crest to scorn the scowling fates,
His legions gather round him and madly charge and cheer,
And fill the besieging armies with wild disheveled fear.

Then bares his breast unto the dart the daring spearsman sends,
And dying hears his cheering foes, the wailing of his friends,
So Albert Sidney Johnston, the chief of belt and scar,
Lay down to die at Shiloh and turned the scales of war.

Now five and twenty years are gone, and lo, today they come,
The Blue and Gray in proud array with throbbing fife and drum;
But not as rivals, not as foes, as brothers reconciled,
To twine love's fragrant roses where the thorns of hate grew wild.

They tell the hero of three wars, the lion-hearted man,
Who wore his valor like a star—uncrowned American;
Above his heart serene and still the folded Stars and Bars,
Above his head like mother-wings, the sheltering Stripes and Stars.

Aye, five and twenty years, and lo, the manhood of the South
Has held its valor stanch and strong as at the cannon's mouth,
With patient heart and silent tongue has kept its true parole,
And in the conquests born of peace has crowned its battle roll.

But ever while we sing of war, of courage tried and true,
Of heroes wed to gallant deeds, or be it Gray or Blue,
Then Albert Sidney Johnston's name shall flash before our sight
Like some resplendent meteor across the sombre night.

America, thy sons are knit with sinews wrought of steel,
They will not bend, they will not break, beneath the tyrant's heel;
But in the white-hot flame of love, to silken cobwebs spun,
They whirl the engines of the world, all keeping time as one.

Today they stand abreast and strong, who stood as foes of yore,
The world leaps up to bless their feet, heaven scatters blessings o'er;
Their robes are wrought of gleaming gold, their wings are freedom's
    own,
The tramping of their conquering hosts shakes pinnacle and throne.

Oh, veterans of the Blue and Gray, who fought on Shiloh field,
The purposes of God are true, His judgment stands revealed;
The pangs of war have rent the veil, and lo, His high decree;
One heart, one hope, one destiny, one flag from sea to sea.

KATE BROWNLEE SHERWOOD

MARTHY VIRGINIA'S HAND

"There, on the left!" said the colonel; the battle had shuddered and faded away,
Wraith of a fiery enchantment that left only ashes and blood-sprinkled clay—
"Ride to the left and examine that ridge, where the enemy's sharpshooters stood.
Lord, how they picked off our men, from the treacherous vantage-ground of the wood!
But for their bullets, I'll bet, my batteries sent them something as good.
Go and explore, and report to me then, and tell me how many we killed.
Never a wink shall I sleep till I know our vengeance was duly fulfilled."

Fiercely the orderly rode down the slope of the cornfield—scarred and forlorn,
Rutted by violent wheels, and scathed by the shot that had ploughed it in scorn;
Fiercely, and burning with wrath for the sight of his comrades crushed at a blow,
Flung in broken shapes on the ground like ruined memorials of woe;
These were the men whom at daybreak he knew, but never again could know.
Thence to the ridge, where roots out-thrust, and twisted branches of trees
Clutched the hill like clawing lions, firm their prey to seize.

"What's your report?" and the grim colonel smiled when the orderly came back at last.
Strangely the soldier paused: "Well, they were punished." And strangely his face looked aghast.
"Yes, our fire told on them; knocked over fifty—laid out in line of parade.
Brave fellows, Colonel, to stay as they did! But one I 'most wished hadn't stayed.
Mortally wounded, he'd torn off his knapsack; and then, at the end, he prayed—
Easy to see, by his hands that were clasped; and the dull, dead fingers yet held
This little letter—his wife's—from the knapsack. A pity those woods were shelled!"

Silent the orderly, watching with tears in his eyes as his officer scanned
Four short pages of writing. "What's this, about 'Marthy Virginia's hand'?"
Swift from his honeymoon he, the dead soldier, had gone from his bride to the strife;
Never they met again, but she had written him, telling of that new life,
Born in the daughter, that bound her still closer and closer to him as his wife.
Laying her baby's hand down on the letter, around it she traced a rude line:
"If you would kiss the baby," she wrote, "you must kiss this outline of mine."

There was the shape of the hand on the page, with the small, chubby fingers outspread.
"Marthy Virginia's hand, for her pa,"—so the words on the little palm said.
Never a wink slept the colonel that night, for the vengeance so blindly fulfilled.

Never again woke the old battle-glow when the bullets their death-note shrilled.
Long ago ended the struggle in union of brotherhood happily stilled;
Yet from that field of Antietam, in warning and token of love's command,
See! there is lifted the hand of a baby—Marthy Virginia's hand!

GEORGE PARSONS LATHROP
(*Virginia*)

KENTUCKY BELLE

Summer of sixty-three, sir, and Conrad was gone away—
Gone to the county-town, sir, to sell our first load of hay—
We lived in the log house yonder, poor as you've ever seen;
Roschen there was a baby, and I was only nineteen.

Conrad, he took the oxen, but he left Kentucky Belle.
How much we thought of Kentuck, I couldn't begin to tell—
Came from the Blue-Grass country; my father gave her to me
When I rode North with Conrad, away from Tennessee.

Conrad lived in Ohio—a German he is, you know—
The house stood in broad cornfields, stretching on, row after row.
The old folks made me welcome; they were kind as kind could be;
But I kept longing, longing, for the hills of Tennessee.

Oh! for a sight of water, the shadowed slope of a hill!
Clouds that hang on the summit, a wind that never is still!
But the level land went stretching away to meet the sky—
Never a rise, from north to south, to rest the weary eye!

From east to west no river to shine out under the moon,
Nothing to make a shadow in the yellow afternoon:
Only the breathless sunshine, as I looked out, all forlorn;
Only the "rustle," as I walked among the corn.

When I fell sick with pining, we didn't wait any more,
But moved away from the corn-lands, out to this river shore—
The Tuscarawas it's called, sir—off there's a hill, you see—
And now I've grown to like it next best to the Tennessee.

I was at work that morning. Some one came riding like mad
Over the bridge and up the road—Farmer Rouf's little lad.
Bareback he rode; he had no hat; he hardly stopped to say,
"Morgan's men are coming, Frau; they're galloping on this way.

"I'm sent to warn the neighbors. He isn't a mile behind;
He sweeps up all the bones—every horse that he can find.
Morgan, Morgan the raider, and Morgan's terrible men,
With bowie-knives and pistols, are galloping up the glen!"

The lad rode down the valley, and I stood still at the door;
The baby laughed and prattled, playing with spools on the floor;
Kentuck was out in the pasture; Conrad, my man was gone.
Near, nearer, Morgan's men were galloping, galloping on!

Sudden I picked up baby, and ran to the pasture-bar.
"Kentuck!" I called—"Kentucky!" She knew me ever so far!
I led her down the gully that turns off there to the right.
And tied her to the bushes; her head was just out of sight.

As I ran back to the log house, at once there came a sound—
The ring of hoofs, galloping hoofs, trembling over the ground—
Coming into the turnpike, out from the White-Woman Glen—
Morgan, Morgan the raider, and Morgan's terrible men.

As near they drew and nearer, my heart beat fast in alarm;
But still I stood in the doorway with baby on my arm.
They came; they passed; with spur and whip in haste they sped
along—
Morgan, Morgan the raider, and his band, six hundred strong.

Weary they looked and jaded, riding through night and through day;
Pushing on East to the river, many long miles away,
To the border-strip where Virginia runs up into the West,
And forcing the Upper Ohio before they could stop to rest.

On like the wind they hurried, and Morgan rode in advance;
Bright were his eyes like live coals, as he gave me a sideways glance;
I was just breathing freely, after my choking pain,
When the last one of the troopers suddenly drew his rein.

Frightened I was to death, sir; I scarce dared look in his face,
As he asked for a drink of water, and glanced around the place.
I gave him a cup and he smiled—'twas only a boy, you see;
Faint and worn, with dim blue eyes; and he'd sailed on the Tennessee.

Only sixteen he was, sir—a fond mother's only son—
Off and away with Morgan before his life has begun!
The damp drops stood on his temples—drawn was the boyish mouth;
And I thought me of the mother waiting down in the South.

Oh! pluck was he to the backbone, and clear grit through and through;
Boasted and bragged like a trooper, but the big words wouldn't do;—
The boy was dying, sir, dying, as plain as plain could be,
Worn out by his ride with Morgan up from the Tennessee.

But when I told the laddie that I, too, was from the South,
Water came in his dim eyes, and quivers around his mouth.
"Do you know the Blue-Grass country?" he wistful began to say;
Then swayed like a willow-sapling and fainted dead away.

I had him into the log house, and worked and brought him to;
I fed him and I coaxed him, as I thought his mother'd do;
And when the lad grew better, and the noise in his head was gone,
Morgan's men were miles away, galloping, galloping on.

"Oh, I must go," he muttered: "I must be up and away!
Morgan—Morgan is waiting for me! Oh, what will Morgan say?"
But I heard a sound of tramping and kept him back from the door—
The ringing sound of horses' hoofs that I had heard before.

And on, on, came the soldiers—the Michigan cavalry—
And fast they rode, and black they looked, galloping rapidly,—
They had followed hard on Morgan's track; they had followed day
and night;
But of Morgan and Morgan's raiders they had never caught a sight.

And rich Ohio sat startled through all those summer days;
For strange, wild men were galloping over her broad highways—
Now here, now there, now seen, now gone, now north, now east,
now west,
Through river-valleys and corn-land farms, sweeping away her
best.

A bold ride and a long ride! But they were taken at last.
They almost reached the river by galloping hard and fast;
But the boys in blue were upon them ere ever they gained the ford,
And Morgan, Morgan the raider, laid down his terrible sword.

Well, I kept the boy till evening—kept him against his will—
But he was too weak to follow, and sat there pale and still.
When it was cool and dusky—you'll wonder to hear me tell—
But I stole down to that gully, and brought up Kentucky Belle.

I kissed the star on her forehead—my pretty gentle lass—
But I knew that she'd be happy back in the old Blue Grass.
A suit of clothes of Conrad's, with all the money I had,
And Kentuck, pretty Kentuck, I gave to the worn-out lad.

I guided him to the southward as well as I knew how;
The boy rode off with many thanks, and many a backward bow;
And then the glow it faded, and my heart began to swell,
As down the glen away she went, my lost Kentucky Belle!

When Conrad came in the evening, the moon was shining high;
Baby and I were both crying—I couldn't tell him why—
But a battered suit of rebel gray was hanging on the wall,
And a thin old horse, with drooping head, stood in Kentucky's stall.

Well, he was kind, and never once said a hard word to me;
He knew I couldn't help it—'twas all for the Tennessee.
But, after the war was over, just think what came to pass—
A letter, sir; and the two were safe back in the old Blue Grass.

The lad had got across the border, riding Kentucky Belle;
And Kentuck she was thriving, and fat, and hearty, and well;
He cared for her, and kept her, nor touched her with whip or spur.
Ah! we've had many horses since, but never a horse like her!

CONSTANCE FENIMORE WOOLSON

(Ohio)

APPOMATTOX

On the death of Grant

To peace-white ashes sunk war's lurid flame;
  The drums had ceased to growl, and died away
  The bark of guns, where fronting armies lay,
And for the day the dogs of war are tame,
And resting on the field of blood-fought fame,
  For peace at last o'er horrid war held sway
  On her won field, a score of years today,
Where to her champion forth a white flag came,
O nation's chief, thine eyes have seen again
  A whiter flag come forth to summon thee

Than that pale scarf which gleamed above war's stain,
To parley o'er the end of its red reign—
  The truce of God that sets from battle free
Thy dauntless soul, and thy worn life from pain.

Ben D. House
(*Indiana*)

THE REVEILLE

Hark! I hear the tramp of thousands,
  And of armed men the hum;
Lo! a nation's hosts have gathered
  Round the quick-alarming drum,—
    Saying: "Come,
    Freemen, come!
Ere your heritage be wasted," said the quick-alarming drum.

"Let me of my heart take counsel;
  War is not of life the sum;
Who shall stay and reap the harvest
  When the autumn days shall come?"
    But the drum
    Echoed: "Come!
Death shall reap the braver harvest," said the solemn-sounding drum.

"But when won the coming battle,
  What of profit springs therefrom?
What if conquest, subjugation,
  Even greater ills become?"
    But the drum
    Answered: "Come!
You must do the sum to prove it," said the Yankee-answering drum.

"What if, 'mid the cannons' thunder,
Whistling shot and bursting bomb
When my brothers fall around me,
Should my heart grow cold and numb?"
But the drum
Answered: "Come!
Better there in death united than in life a recreant,—Come!"

Thus they answered—hoping, fearing,
Some in faith and doubting some,
Till a trumpet-voice proclaiming,
Said: "My chosen people, come!"
Then the drum,
Lo! was dumb;
For the great heart of the nation, throbbing, answered: "Lord, we come!"

BRET HARTE
(California)

THE DAUGHTER OF THE REGIMENT

Who with the soldiers was stanch danger-sharer,—
Marched in the ranks through the shriek of the shell?
Who was their comrade, their brave color-bearer?
Who but the resolute Kady Brownell!

Over the marshland and over the highland,
Where'er the columns wound, meadow or dell,
Fared she, this daughter of little Rhode Island,—
She, the intrepid one, Kady Brownell!

While the mad rout at Manassas was surging,
When those around her fled wildly, or fell,
And the bold Beauregard onward was urging,
Who so undaunted as Kady Brownell!

When gallant Burnside made dash upon Newberne,
  Sailing the Neuse 'gainst the sweep of the swell,
Watching the flag on the heaven's broad blue burn,
  Who higher hearted than Kady Brownell?

In the deep slough of the springtide debarking,
  Toiling o'er leagues that are weary to tell,
Time with the sturdiest soldiery marking,
  Forward, straight forward, strode Kady Brownell.

Reaching the lines where the army was forming,
  Forming to charge on those ramparts of hell,
When from the weed came her regiment swarming,
  What did she see there—this Kady Brownell?

See! why she saw that their friends thought them foemen;
  Muskets were levelled, and cannon as well!
Save them from direful destruction would no men?
  Nay, but this woman would,—Kady Brownell!

Waving her banner she raced for the clearing;
  Fronted them all, with her flag as a spell;
Ah, what a volley—a volley of cheering—
  Greeted the heroine, Kady Brownell!

Gone (and thank God!) are those red days of slaughter!
  Brethren again we in amity dwell;
Just one more cheer for the Regiment's Daughter!—
  Just one more cheer for her, Kady Brownell!

CLINTON SCOLLARD
(*Rhode Island*)

THE PRIDE OF BATTERY B

South Mountain towering on our right,
  Far off the river lay,
And over on the wooded height
  We held their lines at bay.

At last the muttering guns were still,
  The day died slow and wan;
At last the gunners' pipes did fill,
  The sergeant's yarns began.

When, as the wind a moment blew
  Aside the fragrant flood
Our brierwoods raised, within our view
  A little maiden stood.

A tiny tot of six or seven,
  From fireside fresh she seemed
(Of such a little one in heaven
  One soldier often dreamed).

And as we stared, her little hand
  Went to her curly head
In grave salute. "And who are you?"
  At length the sergeant said.

"And where's your home?" He growled again,
  She lisped out, "Who is me?
Why, don't you know? I'm little Jane,
  The pride of Battery B.

"My home? Why, that was burned away,
  And Pa and Ma are dead,
And so I ride the guns all day,
  Along with Sergeant Ned.

"And I've a drum that's not a toy,
A cap with feathers, too,
And I march beside the drummer boy
On Sundays at review.

"But now, our 'bacca's all give out,
The men can't have their smoke.
And so they're cross. Why, even Ned
Won't play with me and joke!

"And the big colonel said today—
I hate to hear him swear—
He'd give a leg for a good pipe
Like the Yank had over there.

"And so I thought, when beat the drum,
And the big guns were still,
I'd creep beneath the tent and come
Down here across the hill,

"And beg, good Master Yankee men,
You give me some Lone Jack,
Please do; when we get some again
I'll surely bring it back.

"Indeed! I will, for Ned, says he,
If I do what I say
I'll be a general yet, maybe,
And ride a prancing bay."

We brimmed her tiny apron o'er;
You should have heard her laugh
And each man from his scanty store
Shook out a generous half!

To kiss the little mouth, stooped down
  A score of grimy men,
Until the sergeant's husky voice
  Said, " 'Tention, squad!" and then

We gave her escort, till good-night
  The pretty waif we bid,
And watched her toddle out of sight
  Or else 'twas tears that hid

Her tiny form—nor turned about
  A man, not spoke a word,
Till after awhile a far, hoarse shout
  Upon the wind we heard.

We sent it back, then cast sad eyes
  Upon the scene around;
A baby's hand had touched the ties
  That brothers once had bound.

That's all—save when the dawn awoke
  Again the work of hell,
And through the sullen clouds of smoke
  The screaming missiles fell.

Our general often rubbed his glass
  And marveled much to see
Not a single shell that whole day fell
  In the camp of Battery B.

AUTHOR UNKNOWN

MISSING

In the cool, sweet hush of a wooded nook,
  Where the May buds sprinkle the green old mound,
And the winds and the birds and the limpid brook,
  Murmur their dreams with a drowsy sound;

Who lies so still in the plushy moss,
With his pale cheek pressed on a breezy pillow,
Couched where the light and the shadows cross
Through the flickering fringe of the willow?
Who lies, alas!
So still, so chill, in the whispering grass?

A soldier clad in the Zouave dress,
A bright-haired man, with his lips apart,
One hand thrown up o'er his frank, dead face,
And the other clutching his pulseless heart,
Lies here in the shadows, cool and dim,
His musket swept by a trailing bough,
With a careless grace in each quiet limb,
And a wound on his manly brow
A wound, alas!
Whence the warm blood drips on the quiet grass.

The violets peer from their dusky beds
With a tearful dew in their great pure eyes;
The lilies quiver their shining heads,
Their pale lips full of a sad surprise;
And the lizard darts through the glistening fern—
And the squirrel rustles the branches hoary;
Strange birds fly out, with a cry, to bathe
Their wings in the sunset glory;
While the shadows pass
O'er the quiet face and the dewy grass.

God pity the bride who waits at home,
With her lily cheeks and her violet eyes,
Dreaming the sweet old dreams of love,
While her lover is walking in Paradise;
God strengthen her heart as the days go by,
And the long, drear nights of her vigil follow,

Nor bird, nor moon, nor whispering wind,
May breathe the tale of the hollow;
Alas! Alas!
The secret is safe with the woodland grass.

AUTHOR UNKNOWN

MY WARRIOR BOY

Thou hast gone forth, my darling one,
To battle with the brave,
To strike in Freedom's sacred cause,
Or win an early grave;
With vet'rans grim, and stalwart men,
Thy pathway lieth now,
Though fifteen summers scarce have shed
Their blossoms on thy brow.

My babe in years, my warrior boy!
Oh, if a mother's tears
Could call thee back to be my joy
And still these anxious fears,
I'd dash the traitor drops away,
That would unnerve thy hand,
Now raised to strike in Freedom's cause
For thy dear native land.

God speed thee on thy course, my boy,
Where'er thy pathway lie,
And guard thee when the leaden hail
Shall thick around thee fly;
But when our sacred cause is won,
And peace again shall reign,
Come back to me, my darling son,
And light my life again.

AUTHOR UNKNOWN

THE BROKEN MUG

My mug is broken, my heart is sad!
  What woes can fate still hold in store
The friend I cherished a thousand days
  Is smashed to pieces on the floor!
  Is shattered and to Limbo gone,
    I'll see my Mug no more!

Relic it was of joyous hours
  Whose golden memories still allure—
When coffee made of rye we drank,
  And gray was all the dress we wore!
When we were paid some cents a month,
  But never asked for more!

In marches long, by day and night,
  In raids, hot charges, shocks of war,
Strapped on the saddle at my back
  This faithful comrade still I bore—
  This old companion, true and tried,
    I'll never carry more!

From the Rapidan to Gettysburg—
  "Hard bread" behind, "sour krout" before—
This friend went with the cavalry
  And heard the jarring cannon roar
  In front of Cemetery Hill—
    Good heavens! how they did roar!

Then back again, the foe behind,
  Back to the "Old Virginia shore"—
Some dead and wounded left—some holes
  In flags, the sullen graybacks bore;
  This mug had made the great campaign,
    And we'd have gone once more!

Alas! we never went again!
  The red cross banner, slow but sure.
"Fell back"—we bade to sour krout
  (Like the lover of Lenore)
  A long, sad, lingering farewell—
    To taste its joys no more.

But still we fought, and ate hard bread,
  Or starved—good friend, our woes deplore
And still this faithful friend remained—
  Riding behind me as before—
  The friend on march, in bivouac,
    When others were no more.

How oft we drove the horsemen blue
  In Summer bright, or Winter frore!
How oft before the Southern charge
  Through field and wood the blue-birds tore!
  I'm "harmonized," but long to hear
    The bugles ring once more.

Oh yes! we're all "fraternal" now,
  Purged of our sins, we're clean and pure,
Congress will "reconstruct" us soon—
  But no gray people on that floor!
  I'm harmonized—"so-called"—but long
    To see those times once more!

Gay days! the sun was brighter then,
  And we were happy, though so poor!
That past comes back as I behold
  My shattered friend upon the floor,
  My splintered, useless, ruined mug,
    From which I'll drink no more.

How many lips I'll love for aye,
  While heart and memory endure.
Have touched this broken cup and laughed—
  How they did laugh!—in days of yore!
  Those days we'd call "a beauteous dream,"
    If they had been no more!

Dear comrades, dead this many a day,
  I saw you weltering in your gore,
After those days amid the pines
  On the Rappahannock shore!
  When the joy of life was much to me
    But your warm hearts were more!

Yours was the grand heroic nerve
  That laughs amid the storm of war—
Souls that "loved much" your native land,
  Who fought and died therefor!
  You gave your youth, your brains, your arms,
    Your blood—you had no more!

You lived and died true to your flag!
  And now your wounds are healed—but sore
Are many hearts that think of you
  Where you have "gone before."
  Peace, comrade! God bound up those forms,
    They are "whole" forevermore!

Those lips this broken vessel touched,
  His, too!—the man's we all adore—
That cavalier of cavaliers,
  Whose voice will ring no more—
  Whose plume will float amid the storm
    Of battle never more!

Not on this idle page I write
  That name of names, shrined in the core
Of every heart!—peace! foolish pen,
  Hush! words so cold and poor!
  His sword is rust; the blue eyes dust,
    His bugle sounds no more!

Never was cavalier like ours!
  Not Rupert in the years before!
And when his stern, hard work was done,
  His griefs, joys, battles o'er—
  His mighty spirit rode the storm,
    And led his men once more!

He lies beneath his native sod,
  Where violets spring, or frost is hoar;
He recks not—charging squadrons watch
  His raven plume no more!
  That smile we'll see, that voice we'll hear,
    That hand we'll touch no more!

My foolish mirth is quenched in tears:
  Poor fragments strewed upon the floor,
Ye are the types of nobler things
  That find their use no more—
  Things glorious once, now trodden down—
    That makes us smile no more!

Of courage, pride, high hopes, stout hearts—
  Hard, stubborn nerve, devotion pure,
Beating his wings against the bars,
  The prisoned eagle tried to soar;
  Outmatched, o'erwhelmed, we struggled still—
    Bread failed—we fought no more!

Lies in the dust the shattered staff
  That bore aloft on sea and shore,
That blazing flag, amid the storm!
  And none are now so poor,
  So poor to do it reverence.
    Now when it flames no more!

But it is glorious in the dust,
  Sacred till Time shall be no more;
Spare it, fierce editors! your scorn—
The dread "Rebellion's" o'er!
  Furl the great flag—hide cross and star,
  Thrust into darkness star and bar,
  But look! across the ages far
    It flames for evermore!

JOHN ESTEN COOKE

THE RAPPAHANNOCK ARMY SONG

The toil of the march is over—
  The pack will be borne no more—
For we've come for the help of Richmond,
  From the Rappahannock's shore.
The foe is closing round us—
  We can hear his ravening cry;
So, ho! for fair old Richmond!
  Like soldiers we'll do or die.

We have left the land that bore us,
  Full many a league away,
And our mothers and sisters miss us,
  As with tearful eyes they pray;
But this will repress their weeping,
  And still the rising sigh—
For all, for fair old Richmond,
  Have come to do or die.

We have come to join our brothers
  From the proud Dominion's vales,
And to meet the dark-cheeked soldier,
  Tanned by the Tropic gales;
To greet them all full gladly,
  With hand and beaming eye,
And to swear for fair old Richmond,
  We all will do or die.

The fair Carolina sisters
  Stand ready, lance in hand,
To fight as they did in an older war,
  For the sake of their fatherland.
The glories of Sumter and Bethel
  Have raised their fame full high,
But they'll fade, if for fair old Richmond
  They swear not to do or die,

Zollicoffer looks down on his people,
  And trusts to their hearts and arms,
To avenge the blood he has shed,
  In the midst of the battle's alarms.
Alabamians, remember the past,
  Be the "South at Manassas," their cry;
As onward for fair old Richmond,
  They marched to do or die.

Brave Bartow, from home on high,
  Calls the Empire State to the front,
To bear once more as she has borne
  With glory the battle's brunt.
Mississippians who know no surrender,
  Bear the flag of the Chief on high;
For he, too, for fair old Richmond,
  Has sworn to do or die.

Fair land of my birth—sweet Florida—
  Your arm is weak, but your soul
Must tell of a purer, holier strength,
  When the drums for the battle roll.
Look within, for your hope in the combat,
  Nor think of your few with a sigh—
If you win not for fair old Richmond,
  At least you can bravely die.

Onward all! Oh! band of brothers!
  The beat of the long roll's heard!
And the hearts of the columns advancing
  By the sound of its music stirred.
Onward all! and never return,
  Till our foes from the borders fly—
To be crowned by the fair of old Richmond,
  As those who could do or die.

JOHN C. M'LEMORE

THE SOLDIER'S AMEN

As a couple of good soldiers were walking one day,
Said one to the other: "Let's kneel down and pray;
I'll pray for the war, and good of all men,
And whatever I pray for, do you say—'Amen!'

"We'll pray for the generals and all of their crew,
Likewise for the captains and lieutenants, too;
May good luck and good fortune them always attend;
And return safely home!" Said the soldier—"Amen!"

"We'll pray for the privates, the noblest of all;
They do all the work and get no glory at all;
May good luck and good fortune them always attend,
And return crowned with laurels!" Said the soldier—"Amen!"

"We'll pray for the pretty boys who want themselves wives,
And have not the courage to strike for their lives;
May bad luck and bad fortune them always attend;
And go down to Old Harry," Said the soldier—"Amen!"

"We'll pray for the pretty girls, who make us good wives,
And always look at a soldier with tears in their eyes;
May good luck and good fortune them always attend,
And brave gallants for sweethearts!" Said the soldier—"Amen!"

"We'll pray for the conscript, with frown on his brow,
To fight for his country he won't take the vow:
May bad luck and bad fortune him always attend,
And die with dishonor!" Said the soldier—"Amen!"

AUTHOR UNKNOWN

CAPTAIN LATANE

The combat raged not long; but ours the day,
And through the hosts which compassed us around
Our little band rode proudly on its way,
Leaving one gallant spirit, glory crowned,
Unburied on the field he died to gain;
Single, of all his men, among the hostile slain!

One moment at the battle's edge he stood,
Hope's halo, like a helmet, round his hair—
The next, beheld him dabbled in his blood,
Prostrate in death; and yet in death how fair!
And thus he passed, through the red gates of strife,
From earthly crowns and palms, to an eternal life.

A brother bore his body from the field,
And gave it into stranger's hands, who closed
His calm blue eyes, on earth forever sealed,
And tenderly the slender limbs composed;
Strangers, but sisters, who with Mary's love,
Sat by the open tomb and, weeping, looked above,

A little girl strewed roses on his bier,
Pale roses—not more stainless than his soul,
Nor yet more fragrant than his life sincere,
That blossomed with good actions—brief, but whole
The aged matron, with the faithful slave,
Approached with reverent steps the hero's lowly grave.

No man of God might read the burial rite
Above the rebel—thus declared the foe,
Who blanched before him in the deadly fight;
But woman's voice, in accents soft and low,
Trembling with pity, touched with pathos, read
Over his hallowed dust, the ritual for the dead!

" 'Tis sown in weakness; it is raised in power."
Soft the promise floated on the air,
And the sweet breathings of the sunset hour,
Come back responsive to the mourner's prayer.
Gently they laid him underneath the sod,
And left him with his fame, his country and his God.

We should not weep for him! His deeds endure;
So young, so beautiful, so brave—he died
As he would wish to die. The past secure,
Whatever yet of sorrow may betide
Those who still linger by the stormy shore;
Change cannot hurt him now, nor fortune reach him more

And when Virginia, leaning on her spear,
Victrix et vidua, the conflict done,
Shall raise her mailed hand to wipe the tear
That starts, as she recalls each martyr son;
No prouder memory her breast shall sway
Than thine—the early lost—lamented Latane!

JOHN R. THOMPSON
(*Virginia*)

AT LEXINGTON

All day a pilgrim had I gone
Across Virginia's storied land,
The lure of "Lexington!"
Leading me ever on.
What though the land in ruins lay?
The autumn fields cropless and gray?—
From far and near that day
Undaunted mid defeat and shame,
The South's young manhood came,
No more at war's, but duty's proud command.

But night was now at hand,
And weary, travel-stained I stood
And from a hilltop's fringe of wood
On straggling spires and homes looked down.
And could it be, this little town,
The goal of life's dream-years?
Almost it moved to bitter tears
Such close should be to youth's glad quest.
And still I lingered by the way,
While fancy yearned to make the best
Of all that eye could see:
Close round the guardian mountains pressed;
Northward, the river darkling flowed;
And near, in cloistral quiet showed
Those dreamed-of pillared walls, aglow
With the last light of day;
And there below,
Shadowed by many a tree,
The tomb of Lee.
O river, hills, and town,—that name
Has crowned you with a crown of flame!

To doubt and linger more what need?
Now to your longings give all speed,

O pilgrim. Yet 'twere meet
To go with naked feet,
For sacred is the ground you tread.
Around you are the mighty dead;
And where yon clustering marble gleams
Faint in the rising moon's first beams,
Great Stonewall sleeps his victor sleep.
But wander past and let him keep
His glory still a while unsung.
Blest was he that he died so young,—
So young the cause he glorified.
What if defeat had tried
That stern sad soul's unyielding pride?—
Victor he lived, victor he died.
Some day, O Muses, hither bring
Poet worthy his deeds to sing.

Yet victory
Alone makes not the great;
But victor over fate
Itself was Lee,
Who made defeat his perfect fame,
And taught us what the great may be.
Oh, holy are this hill and wood,
For here perhaps it was he stood,
When on that August day he came,
And gazed with kingly eyes upon
His little realm of Lexington.
Oh, not in vain
The waiting of those patient days,
When from the jeering world apart,
Wandering in lonely ways,
You nursed the promise in your heart!
Deep in untroubled haunts of pine,
On fragrant needles stretched supine,
Reading the tales all but divine

As that divinest tale of long ago
Of Hector's might and Ilion's woe,—
Time's latest page of chivalry:
Grim Stonewall and his Ironsides,
Pickett's charge, and Stuart's rides,
And everywhere the soul of Lee.

But linger not, for nigh at hand
Moonlit and ivy-mantled stand
The chapel walls, and on the floor,
From oriel windows silvered o'er
With moonlight's unstained glory, see
  The tomb of Lee.

Your pilgrimage at last is done:
The goal of life's dream-years is won!

Is it enough, enough, to stand
With duly folded hand
And reverent-bended head!
Kneel down and to the marble lay
Your lips and humbly pay
Meet reverence to the dead.
And he whose hand had hurled
The thunderbolt and all but riven
The land in twain and given
Another nation to the world—
Put on the scholar's cap and gown:
Not worn as martyr's robe and crown
But with a high humility
Which taught us what the great can be.

But hasten down; and leave the throng
To their own boyish ways, of song
And laughter. What have you,
O pilgrim, yet with these to do!

Still is your pilgrimage undone.
Each roving band of comrades shun;
Down the dim street untended make,
Till from its lordly hilltop, bright
As a vision in the moon's full light,
The wide old pillared front shall break
  Right on your startled gaze:
    At last! At last!
Oh, not in vain
The yearnings of those unblest days
Forever now behind you cast!
For to a boy's untutored dreams
As grand the humble vision seems
As when of old a festal train
From far off isle amid the main,
Landing at holy Marathon,
Over Pentelicus all day have gone,
At sunset gain
Hymettus and the Attic plain,
  And silently look down upon
  The Parthenon! The Parthenon!

Good is it to be here.
O pilgrim, what have you to fear?
Though slowly hence the moonbeams glide
And all grows dark, and at your side
An awful presence stands.
Fear not, but mutely lift
Your suppliant hands
And beg the longed-for gift:—
Some day to come and lay
Tribute of deathless song—
Voiced alike by friends and foes—
Upon his tomb and somewhat pay
The debt a nation owes.—

(Oh, Chieftain, it was long,
So long ago, the gift I prayed,
And daily have my lips essayed
To keep the vow which then they made;
But toil and time work grievous wrong,
Stealing away the poet fire
And leaving but unquenched desire.
My chieftain, on your tomb today
Tribute of song I lay:
Not what I would but what I may.)

But now a waking bird has cried
"The dawn! the dawn!" O pilgrim, rise
And hasten forth and take your place
Your toiling brother-man beside,
A new day's radiance on your face,
A new day's promise in your eyes.

And leave your Chieftain to his sleep:
  His very name
  Time's self will keep
  In sacred trust.
Out of war's ruin, wrong, and shame,—
  Just or unjust,—
The work of peace that here he wrought,
The patient, far-off ends he sought,
His ever-brightening star of fame,
In the long years to be,—
Our stern, high task before us set,
Our hands in love and duty met,—
Will lead his people yet
  To victory.

BENJAMIN SLEDD
(*North Carolina*)

CHARLESTON

(*February, 1865*)

Calmly beside her tropic strand,
  An empress, brave and loyal,
I see the watchful city stand,
  With aspect sternly royal;
She knows her mortal foe draws near,
  Armored by subtlest science,
Yet deep, majestical, and clear,
  Rings out her grand defiance.
Oh, glorious is thy noble face,
  Lit up by proud emotion,
And unsurpassed thy stately grace,
  Our warrior Queen of Ocean!

First from thy lips the summons came,
  Which roused our South to action,
And, with the quenchless force of flame,
  Consumed the demon, Faction;
First, like a rush of sovereign wind,
  That rends dull waves asunder,
Thy prescient warning struck the blind,
  And woke the deaf with thunder;
They saw, with swiftly kindling eyes,
  The shameful doom before them,
And heard, borne wild from northern skies,
  The death-gale hurtling o'er them:

Wilt thou, whose virgin banner rose,
  A morning star of splendor,
Quail when the war-tornado blows,
  And crouch in base surrender?
Wilt thou, upon whose loving breast
  Our noblest chiefs are sleeping,
Yield thy dead patriots' place of rest
  To scornful alien keeping?

No! while a life-pulse throbs for fame,
  Thy sons will gather round thee,
Welcome the shot, the steel, the flame,
  If honor's hand hath crowned thee.

Then fold about thy beauteous form
  The imperial robe thou wearest,
And front with regal port the storm
  Thy foe would dream thou fearest;
If strength, and will, and courage fail
  To cope with ruthless numbers,
And thou must bend, despairing, pale,
  Where thy last hero slumbers,
Lift the red torch, and light the fire
  Amid those corpses gory,
And on thy self-made funeral pyre,
  Pass from the world to glory.

PAUL HAMILTON HAYNE
(*South Carolina*)

THE LONE SENTRY

'Twas in the dying of the day,
  The darkness grew so still;
The drowsy pipe of evening birds
  Was hushed upon the hill;
Athwart the shadows of the vale
  Slumbered the men of might,
And one lone sentry paced his rounds,
  To watch the camp that night.

A grave and solemn man was he,
  With deep and sombre brow;
The dreamful eyes seemed hoarding up
  Some unaccomplished vow.

The wistful glance peered o'er the plains
  Beneath the starry light,
And with the murmured name of God,
  He watched the camp that night.

The Future opened unto him
  Its grand and awful scroll:
Manassas and the Valley march
  Came heaving o'er his soul;
Richmond and Sharpsburg thundered by
  With that tremendous fight
Which gave him to the angel hosts
  Who watched the camp that night.

We mourn for him who died for us
  With one resistless moan;
While up the valley of the Lord
  He marches to the Throne!
He kept the faith of men and saints
  Sublime, and pure, and bright—
He sleeps—and all is well with him
  Who watched the camp that night.

Brothers! the Midnight of the Cause
  Is shrouded in our fate;
The demon Goths pollute our halls
  With fire, and lust, and hate.
Be strong—be valiant—be assured—
  Strike home for Heaven and Right!
The soul of Jackson stalks abroad,
  And guards the camp tonight.

James R. Randall

LEE TO THE REAR

(*May 6, 1864*)

Dawn of a pleasant morning in May
Broke through the Wilderness cool and gray;
While perched in the tallest tree-top, the birds
Were carolling Mendelssohn's "Songs without Words."

Far from the haunts of men remote,
The brook brawled on with a liquid note;
And Nature, all tranquil and lovely, wore
The smile of the spring, as in Eden of yore.

Little by little, as daylight increased,
And deepened the roseate flush in the East—
Little by little did morning reveal
Two long glittering lines of steel;

Where two hundred thousand bayonets gleam,
Tipped with the light of the earliest beam,
And the faces are sullen and grim to see
In the hostile armies of Grant and Lee.

All of a sudden, ere rose the sun,
Pealed on the silence the opening gun—
A little white puff of smoke there came,
And anon the valley was wreathed in flame.

Down on the left of the Rebel lines,
Where a breastwork stands in a copse of pines,
Before the Rebels their ranks can form,
The Yankees have carried the place by storm.

Stars and Stripes on the salient wave,
Where many a hero has found a grave,
And the gallant Confederates strive in vain
The ground they have drenched with their blood, to regain.

Yet louder the thunder of battle roared—
Yet a deadlier fire on the columns poured;
Slaughter infernal rode with Despair,
Furies twain, through the murky air.

Not far off, in the saddle there sat
A gray-bearded man in a black slouched hat;
Not much moved by the fire was he,
Calm and resolute Robert Lee.

Quick and watchful he kept his eye
On the bold Rebel brigades close by,—
Reserves that were standing (and dying) at ease,
While the tempest of wrath toppled over the trees.

For still with their loud, deep, bull-dog bay,
The Yankee batteries blazed away,
And with every murderous second that sped
A dozen brave fellows, alas! fell dead.

The grand old graybeard rode to the space
Where Death and his victims stood face to face,
And silently waved his old slouched hat—
A world of meaning there was in that!

"Follow me! Steady! We'll save the day!"
This was what he seemed to say;
And to the light of his glorious eye
The bold brigades thus made reply:

"We'll go forward, but you must go back"—
And they moved not an inch in the perilous track:
"Go to the rear, and we'll send them to hell!"
And the sound of the battle was lost in their yell.

Turning his bridle, Robert Lee
Rode to the rear. Like waves of the sea,
Bursting the dikes in their overflow,
Madly his veterans dashed on the foe.

And backward in terror that foe was driven,
Their banners rent and their columns riven
Wherever the tide of battle rolled
Over the Wilderness, wood and wold.

Sunset out of a crimson sky
Streamed o'er a field of ruddier dye,
And the brook ran on with a purple stain,
From the blood of ten thousand foemen slain.

Seasons have passed since that day and year—
Again o'er its pebbles the brook runs clear,
And the field in a richer green is drest
Where the dead of a terrible conflict rest.

Hushed is the roll of the Rebel drum,
The sabres are sheathed, and the cannon are dumb;
And Fate, with his pitiless hand, has furled
The flag that once challenged the gaze of the world;

But the fame of the Wilderness fight abides;
And down into history grandly rides,
Calm and unmoved as in battle he sat,
The gray-bearded man in the black slouched hat.

John Reuben Thompson

A SECOND REVIEW OF THE GRAND ARMY

(*May 24, 1865*)

I read last night of the Grand Review
  In Washington's chiefest avenue,—
Two hundred thousand men in blue,
  I think they said was the number,—
Till I seemed to hear their trampling feet,
The bugle blast and the drum's quick beat,
The clatter of hoofs in the stony street,
The cheers of people who came to greet,
And the thousand details that to repeat
  Would only my verse encumber,—
Till I fell in a revery, sad and sweet,
  And then to a fitful slumber.

When, lo! in a vision I seemed to stand
In the lonely Capitol. On each hand
Far stretched the portico, dim and grand
Its columns ranged, like a martial band
Of sheeted spectres, whom some command
  Had called to a last reviewing.
And the streets of the city were white and bare;
No footfall echoed across the square;
But out of the misty midnight air
I heard in the distance a trumpet blare,
And the wandering night-winds seemed to bear
  The sound of a far tattooing.

Then I held my breath with fear and dread;
For into the square, with a brazen tread,
There rode a figure whose stately head
  O'erlooked the review that morning,
That never bowed from its firm-set seat
When the living column passed its feet,
Yet now rode steadily up the street
  To the phantom bugle's warning:

Till it reached the Capitol square, and wheeled,
And there in the moonlight stood revealed
A well-known form that in State and field
  Had led our patriot sires:
Whose face was turned to the sleeping camp,
Afar through the river's fog and damp,
That showed no flicker, nor waning lamp,
  Nor wasted bivouac fires.

And I saw a phantom army come,
With never a sound of fife or drum,
But keeping time to a throbbing hum
  Of wailing and lamentation:
The martyred heroes of Malvern Hill,
Of Gettysburg and Chancellorsville,
The men whose wasted figures fill
  The patriot graves of the nation.

And there came the nameless dead,—the men
Who perished in fever-swamp and fen,
The slowly-starved of the prison-pen;
  And, marching beside the others,
Came the dusky martyrs of Pillow's fight,
With limbs enfranchised and bearing bright:
I thought—perhaps 'twas the pale moonlight—
  They looked as white as their brothers!

And so all night marched the Nation's dead,
With never a banner above them spread,
Nor a badge, nor a motto brandished;
No mark—save the bare uncovered head
  Of the silent bronze Reviewer;
With never an arch save the vaulted sky;
With never a flower save those that lie
On the distant graves—for love could buy
  No gift that was purer or truer.

So all night long swept the strange array;
So all night long, till the morning gray,
I watch'd for one who had passed away,
With a reverent awe and wonder,—
Till a blue cap waved in the lengthening line,
And I knew that one who was kin of mine
Had come; and I spake—and lo! that sign
Awakened me from my slumber.

BRET HARTE
(*California*)

THE COAT OF FADED GRAY

A low hut rests in Lookout's shade,
As rots its moss-grown roof away,
While sundown's glories softly fade,
Closing another weary day.
The battle's din is heard no more,
No more the hunted stand at bay,
The breezes through the lowly door
Swing mute a coat of faded gray,
A tattered relic of the fray,
A threadbare coat of faded gray.

'Tis hanging on the rough log wall,
Near to the foot of a widow's bed,
By a white plume and well-worn shawl—
His gift the happy morn they wed;
By the wee slip their dead child wore—
The one they gave the name of May:
By her rag doll and pinafore—
By right 'tis here that coat of gray
A red-fleck'd relic of the fray,
An armless coat of faded gray.

Her all of life now drapes that wall;
But poor and patient, still she waits
On God's good time to gently call
  Her, too, within the jewell'd gates;
And all she craves is here to die—
  To part from these and pass away,
To join her love eternally
  That wore that—the coat of gray,
    The shell-torn relic of the fray
    Her soldier's coat of faded gray.

G. W. Harris

CONFEDERATE MEMORIAL DAY

The marching armies of the past,
  Along our Southern plains,
Are sleeping now in quiet rest
  Beneath the Southern rains.

The bugle call is now in vain
  To rouse them from their bed;
To arms they'll never march again—
  They are sleeping with the dead.

No more will Shiloh's plains be stained
  With blood our heroes shed,
Nor Chancellorsville resound again
  To our noble warriors' tread.

For them no more shall reveille
  Sound at the break of dawn,
But may their sleep peaceful be
  Till God's great judgment morn.

We bow our heads in solemn prayer
  For those who wore the gray,
And clasp again their unseen hands
  On our Memorial Day.

Author Unknown

CAPTIVES GOING HOME

No flaunting banners o'er them wave,
  No arms flash back the sun's bright ray,
No shouting crowds around them throng,
  No music cheers them on their way;
They're going homc. By adverse fatc
  Compelled their trusty swords to sheathe;
True soldiers they, even though disarmed—
  Heroes, though robbed of victory's wreath.

Brave Southrons! 'Tis with sorrowing hearts
  We gaze upon them through our tears,
And sadly feel how vain were all
  Their heroic deeds through weary years;
Yet, 'mid their enemies they move
  With firm, bold step and dauntless mien;
Oh, Liberty! in every age,
  Such have thy chosen heroes been.

Going home! Alas, to them the words
  Bring visions fraught with gloom and woe:
Since last they saw those cherished homes
  The legions of the invading foe
Have swept them, simoon-like, along,
  Spreading destruction with the wind!
"They found a garden, but they left
  A howling wilderness behind."

Ah! in those desolated homes
  To which the "fate of war has come,"
Sad is the welcome—poor the feast—
  Yet loving ones will round him throng,
With smiles more tender, if less gay,
  And joy will brighten pallid cheeks
  At sight of the dear boys in gray.

Aye, give them welcome home, fair South,
  For you they've made a deathless name;
Bright through all after-time will glow
  The glorious record of their fame.
They made a nation. What, though soon
  Its radiant sun has seemed to set;
The past has shown what they can do,
  The future holds bright promise yet.

AUTHOR UNKNOWN

ONLY A SOLDIER'S GRAVE

Only a soldier's grave! Pass by,
For soldiers, like other mortals, die.
Parents hc had—they are far away;
No sister weeps o'er the soldier's clay;
No brother comes, with a tearful eye:
It's only a soldier's grave—pass by.

True, he was loving, and young, and brave,
Though no glowing epitaph honors his grave;
No proud recital of virtues known,
Of griefs endured, or of triumphs won;
No tablet of marble, or obelisk high;—
Only a soldier's grave—pass by.

Yet bravely he wielded his sword in fight,
And he gave his life in the cause of right!
When his hope was high, and his youthful dream
As warm as the sunlight on yonder stream;
His heart unvexed by sorrow or sigh;—
Yet, 'tis only a soldier's grave:—pass by.

Yet, should we mark it—the soldier's grave,
Some one may seek him in hope to save!
Some of the dear ones, far away,

Would bear him home to his native clay;
'Twere sad, indeed, should they wander nigh,
Find not the hillock, and pass him by.

MAJ. S. A. JONAS
(*Mississippi*)

ENLISTED TODAY

I know the sun shines, and the lilacs are blowing,
And summer sends kisses by beautiful May—
Oh! to see all the treasures the spring is bestowing,
And think my boy Willie enlisted today,

It seems but a day since at twilight, low humming,
I rocked him to sleep with his cheek upon mine,
While Robby, the four-year old, watched for the coming
Of father, adown the street's indistinct line.

It is many a year since my Harry departed,
To come back no more in the twilight or dawn:
And Robby grew weary of watching, and started
Alone on the journey his father had gone.

It is many a year—and this afternoon sitting
At Robby's old window, I heard the band play,
And suddenly ceased dreaming over my knitting,
To recollect Willie is twenty today.

And that, standing beside him this soft May-day morning,
And the sun making gold of his wreathed cigar smoke,
I saw in his sweet eyes and lips a faint warning,
And choked down the tears when he eagerly spoke:

"Dear mother, you know how these Northmen are crowing,
They would trample the rights of the South in the dust,
The boys are all fire; and they wish I were going—"
He stopped, but his eyes said, "Oh, say if I must!"

I smiled on the boy, though my heart it seemed breaking,
  My eyes filled with tears, so I turned them away,
And answered him, "Willie, 'tis well you are waking—
  Go, act as your father would bid you, today!"

I sit in the window, and see the flags flying,
  And drearily list to the roll of the drum,
And smother the pain in my heart that is lying
  And bid all the fears in my bosom be dumb.

I shall sit in the window when summer is lying
  Out over the fields, and the honey-bee's hum
Lulls the rose at the porch from her tremulous sighing,
  And watch for the face of my darling to come.

And if he should fall—his young life he has given
  For freedom's sweet sake; and for me, I will pray
Once more with my Harry and Robby in Heaven
  To meet the dear boy that enlisted today.

AUTHOR UNKNOWN

JUST BEFORE THE BATTLE, MOTHER

Just before the battle, mother,
  I am thinking most of you,
While upon the field we're watching,
  With the enemy in view.
Comrades brave are round me lying,
  Filled with tho'ts of home and God:
For well they know that on the morrow
  Some will sleep beneath the sod.

CHORUS

Farewell, mother, you may never, you may never, mother,
  Press me to your heart again;
But oh, you'll not forget me, mother, you will not forget me.
  If I'm numbered with the slain.

Hark! I hear the bugles sounding,
'Tis the signal for the fight;
Now may God protect us, mother,
As he ever does the right.
Hear the "Battle Cry of Freedom,"
How it swells upon the air;
Oh, yes, we'll rally round the standard,
Or we'll perish nobly there.

CHORUS

G. F. Root

THE DYING SOLDIER BOY

Upon Manassa's bloody plain a soldier boy lay dying!
The gentle winds above his form, in softest tones were sighing;
The god of day had slowly sunk beneath the verge of day,
And the silver moon was gliding above the Milky way.

The stars were shining brightly, and the sky was calm and blue;
Oh! what a beautiful scene was this for human eyes to view;
The river rolled in splendor, and the wavelets danc'd around
But the banks were strewed with dead men, and gory was the ground.

But the hero boy was dying, and his thoughts were very deep,
For the death-wound in his young side was wafting him to sleep.
He thought of home and kindred away on a distant shore,
All of whom he must relinquish, and never see them more.

And as the breeze passed by, in whispers o'er the dead,
Sweet memories of olden days came rushing to his head;
But his mind was weak and deaden'd, so he turned over where he lay,
As the Death Angel flitted by, and called his soul away!

A. B. Cunningham
(*Louisiana*)

THE SOLDIER IN THE RAIN

Ah me! the rain has a sadder sound
  Than it ever had before;
And the wind more plaintively whistles through
  The crevices of the door.

We know we are safe beneath our roof
  From every drop that falls;
And we feel secure and blest, within
  The shelter of our walls.

Then why do we dread to hear the noise
  Of the rapid, rushing rain—
And the plash of the wintry drops, that beat
  Through the blinds, on the window-pane?

We think of the tents on the lowly ground,
  Where our patriot soldiers lie;
And the sentry's bleak and lonely march,
  'Neath the dark and starless sky.

And we pray, with a tearful heart, for those
  Who brave for us yet more—
And we wish this war, with its thousand ills
  And griefs, was only o'er.

We pray when the skies are bright and clear,
  When the winds are soft and warm—
But, oh! we pray with an aching heart
  'Mid the winter's rain and storm.

We fain would lift these mantling clouds
  That shadow our sunny clime;
We can but wait—for we know there'll be
  A day, in the coming time,

When peace, like a rosy dawn, will flood
  Our land with softest light;
Then—we will scarcely hearken the rain
  In the dreary winter's night.

JULIA L. KEYES

MARCHING ALONG

The army is gathering from near and from far,
  The trumpet is sounding the call for the war;
McClellan's our leader, he's gallant and strong,
  We'll gird on our armor and be marching along.

CHORUS

Marching along, we are marching along,
  Gird on the armor and be marching along;
McClellan's our leader, he's gallant and strong,
  For God and our country we are marching along.

The foe is before us in battle array,
  But let us not waver, or turn from the way;
The Lord is our strength, and the Union's our song,
  With courage and faith we are marching along.

CHORUS

Our wives and children we leave in your care,
  We feel you will help them their sorrows to bear;
'Tis hard thus to part, but we hope 'twont be long,
  We'll keep up our hearts as we're marching along.

CHORUS

We sigh for our country, we mourn for our dead,
  For them now our last drop of blood we will shed;
Our cause is the right one—our foe's in the wrong,
  Then gladly we'll sing as we're marching along.

CHORUS

The flag of our country is floating on high,
  We'll stand by that flag till we conquer or die;
McClellan's our leader, he's gallant and strong,
  We'll gird on our armor and be marching along.

CHORUS

WILLIAM B. BRADBURY

OBSEQUIES OF STUART

(*May 12, 1864*)

We could not pause, while yet the noontide air
  Shook with the cannonade's incessant pealing,
The funeral pageant fitly to prepare—
  A nation's grief revealing.

The smoke, above the glimmering woodland wide
  That skirts our southward border in its beauty,
Marked where our heroes stood and fought and died
  For love and faith and duty.

And still, what time the doubtful strife went on,
  We might not find expression for our sorrow;
We could but lay our dear dumb warrior down,
  And gird us for the morrow.

One weary year agone, when came a lull
  With victory in the conflict's stormy closes,
When the glad Spring, all flushed and beautiful,
  First mocked us with her roses,

With dirge and bell and minute-gun, we paid
  Some few poor rites—an inexpressive token
Of a great people's pain—to Jackson's shade,
  In agony unspoken.

No wailing trumpet and no tolling bell,
  No cannon, save the battle's boom receding,
When Stuart to the grave we bore, might tell,
  With hearts all crushed and bleeding.

The crisis suited not with pomp, and she
  Whose anguish bears the seal of consecration
Had wished his Christian obsequies should be
  Thus void of ostentation.

Only the maidens came, sweet flowers to twine
  Above his form so still and cold and painless,
Whose deeds upon our brightest records shine,
  Whose life and sword were stainless.

They well remembered how he loved to dash
  Into the fight, festooned from summer bowers;
How like a fountain's spray his sabre's flash
  Leaped from a mass of flowers.

And so we carried to his place of rest
  All that of our great Paladin was mortal:
The cross, and not the sabre, on his breast,
    That opes the heavenly portal.

No more of tribute might to us remain:
  But there will still come a time when Freedom's martyrs
A richer guerdon of renown shall gain
  Than gleams in stars and garters.

I hear from out that sunlit land which lies
  Beyond these clouds that gather darkly o'er us,
The happy sounds of industry arise
  In swelling peaceful chorus.

And mingling with these sounds, the glad acclaim
  Of millions undisturbed by war's afflictions,
Crowning each martyr's never-dying name
  With grateful benedictions.

In some fair future garden of delights,
  Where flowers shall bloom and song-birds sweetly warble,
Art shall erect the statues of our knights
  In living bronze and marble.

And none of all that bright heroic throng
  Shall wear to far-off time a semblance grander,
Shall still be decked with fresher wreaths of song,
  Than this beloved commander.

The Spanish legend tells us of the Cid,
  That after death he rode, erect, sedately,
Along his lines, even as in life he did,
  In presence yet more stately;

And thus our Stuart, at this moment, seems
  To ride out of our dark and troubled story
Into the region of romance and dreams,
  A realm of light and glory;

And sometimes, when the silver bugles blow,
  That ghostly form, in battle reappearing,
Shall lead his horsemen headlong on the foe,
  In victory careering!

John Reuben Thompson

A CHRISTMAS OF LONG AGO

I am thinking tonight in sadness
  Of a Christmas of long ago,
When the air was filled with gladness,
  And the earth was wrapped in snow;
When the stars like diamonds glistened
  And the night was crisp and cold,
As I eagerly watched and listened
  For the Santa Claus of old.

The forest was robbed of its treasures,
  The house was a mass of green,
And I reveled in Christmas pleasures,
  At the dawn of Aurora's sheen;
Some talked of the Savior's mission,
  But I of my pretty toys;
Some knelt in devout petition—
  I romped and played with the boys.

We went to the pond for skating,
  To the stable to take a ride,
And we found new joys awaiting,
  To whatever spot we hied;
But the climax of my story
  Was that evening's fireworks show!
Went out in a blaze of glory—
  That Christmas of long ago!

But in sadness I think of that Christmas,
  For many then happy and gay
Have gone to the realm of silence
  And sleep in their beds of clay;
The hands that filled kindly my stockings,
  I shall grasp in this world no more,
But when at Heaven's portals I'm knocking
  They'll open the beautiful door.

They will lead me in tenderness clinging,
And place me before the throne,
Where the choirs angelic are singing
And the heavenly gifts are strown,
And there in the realm of glory,
With my loved ones at my side,
I'll repeat the old Bethlehem story
And join in that Christmas tide.

MORTON BRYAN WHARTON, D.D.

THE LITTLE SOLDIER

"When I'm big I'll be a soldier—
That's what I'll be;
Fight for father, fight for mother,
Over land and sea!"
And before him on the table
Stood in bright array
All his little wooden soldiers,
Ready for the fray.
Then he charged his little cannon,
Singing out in glee,
"When I'm big I'll be a soldier—
That's what I will be!"

By the firelight sat the mother;
Tears were in her heart,
Thinking of the swift time coming
When they two must part.

* * * * * *

Soon the shadow fell between them—
Soon the years flew by;
He has left his little mother—
Left her, perhaps to die.

All the laughter gone forever,
  All the sunshine fled;
Only little mother praying
  By his empty bed.

Then there came a dreadful battle,
  And upon the plain
Crept the little mother, seeking
  Some one 'mid the slain;
But she never found her darling
  In the white moon gleam,

For the little cannon firing
  Woke her from her dream.
All a dream! He stood beside her,
  Singing out with glee,
"When I'm big I'll be a soldier—
  That's what I will be!"

J. L. Molloy

GARFIELD'S RIDE AT CHICKAMAUGA

(*September 20, 1863*)

Again the summer-fevered skies,
  The breath of autumn calms;
Again the golden moons arise
  On harvest-happy farms,
The locusts pipe the crickets sing
  Among the falling leaves,
And wandering breezes sigh, and bring
  The harp-notes of the sheaves.

Peace smiles upon the hills and dells;
  Peace smiles upon the seas;
And drop the notes of happy bells
  Upon the fruited trees.

The broad Missouri stretches far
  Her commerce-gathering arms,
And multiply on Arkansas
  The grain-encumbered farms.

Old Chattanooga, crowned with green,
  Sleeps 'neath her walls in peace;
The Argo has returned again,
  And brings the Golden Fleece.
O nation! free from sea to sea,
  In union blessed forever,
Fair be their fame who fought for thee
  By Chickamauga River.

The autumn winds were piping low,
  Beneath the vine-clad eaves;
We heard the hollow bugle blow
  Among the ripened sheaves.
And fast the mustering squadrons passed
  Through mountain portals wide,
And swift the blue brigades were massed
  By Chickamauga's tide.

It was the Sabbath; and in awe
  We heard the dark hills shake,
And o'er the mountain turrets saw
  The smoke of battle break.
And 'neath the war-cloud gray and grand,
  The hills o'erchanging low,
The Army of the Cumberland,
  Unequal, met the foe!

Again, O fair September night!
  Beneath the moon and stars,
I see, through memories dark and bright,
  The altar-fires of Mars.

The morning breaks with screaming guns
From batteries dark and dire,
And where the Chickamauga runs
Red runs the muskets' fire.

I see bold Longstreet's darkening host
Sweep through our lines of flame,
And hear again, "The right is lost!"
Swart Rosecrans exclaim.
"But not the left!" young Garfield cries;
"From that we must not sever,
While Thomas holds the field that lies
On Chickamauga River!"

Oh! on that day of clouded gold,
How, half of hope bereft,
The cannoneers, like Titans, rolled
Their thunders on the left!
I see the battle-clouds again,
With glowing autumn splendors blending:
It seemed as if the gods with men
Were on Olympian heights contending.

Through tongues of flame, through meadows brown,
Dry valley roads concealed,
Ohio's hero dashes down
Upon the rebel field.
And swift, on reeling charger borne,
He threads the wooded plain,
By twice a hundred cannon mown,
And reddened with the slain.

But past swathes of carnage dire,
The Union guns he hears,
And gains the left, begirt with fire,
And thus the heroes cheers—

"While stands the left, yon flag o'erhead,
  Shall Chattanooga stand!"
"Let the Napoleons rain their lead!"
  Was Thomas's command.

Back swept the gray brigades of Bragg;
  The air with victory rung;
And Wurzel's "Rally round the flag!"
  'Mid Union cheers was sung.
The flag on Chattanooga's height
  In twilight's crimson waved,
And all the clustered stars of white
  Were to the Union saved.

O chief of staff! the nation's fate
  That red field crossed with thee,
The triumph of the camp and state,
  The hope of liberty!
O nation! free from sea to sea,
  With union blessed forever,
Not vainly heroes fought for thee
  By Chickamauga River.

In dreams I stand beside the tide
  Where those old heroes fell:
Above the valleys long and wide
  Sweet rings the Sabbath bell.
I hear no more the bugle blow,
  As on that fateful day!
I hear the ringdove fluting low,
  Where shaded waters stray.

On Mission Ridge the sunlight streams
  Above the fields of fall,
And Chattanooga calmly dreams
  Beneath her mountain-wall.

Old Lookout Mountain towers on high,
  As in heroic days,
When 'neath the battle in the sky
  Were seen its summits blaze.

'T was ours to lay no garlands fair
  Upon the graves "unknown":
Kind Nature sets her gentians there,
  And fall the sear leaves lone.
Those heroes' graves no shaft of Mars
  May mark with beauty ever;
But floats the flag of forty stars
  By Chickamauga River.

HEZEKIAH BUTTERWORTH
(Ohio)

CLOUDS IN THE WEST

Hark! on the wind that whistles from the West
  A manly shout for instant succor comes,
From men who fight, outnumbered, breast to breast,
  With rage-indented drums!

Who dare for child, wife, country—stream and strand,
  Though but a fraction to the swarming foe,
There—at the flooded gateways of the land,
  To stem a torrent's flow.

To arms! brave sons of each embattled State,
  Whose queenly standard is a Southern star;
Who would be free must ride the lists of Fate
  On Freedom's victor-car!

Forsake the field, the shop, the mart, the hum
  Of craven traffic for the mustering clan;
The dead themselves are pledged that you shall come
  And prove yourself—a man.

That sacred turf where first a thrilling grief
  Was felt which taught you Heaven alone disposes—
God! can you live to see a foreign thief
  Contaminate its roses?

Blow, summoning trumpets, a compulsive stave,
  Through all the bounds, from Beersheba to Dan;
Come out! come out! who scorns to be a slave,
  Or claims to be a man!

Hark! on the breezes whistling from the West
  A manly shout for instant succor comes,
From men who fight, outnumbered, breast to breast,
  With rage-indented drums!

Who charge and cheer amid the murderous din,
  Where still your battle-flags unbended wave,
Dying for what your fathers died to win
  And you must fight to save.

Ho! shrilly fifes that stir the vales from sleep,
  Ho! brazen thunders from the mountains hoar;
The very waves are marshaling on the deep,
  While tempests tread the shore.

Arise and swear, your palm-engirdled land
  Shall burial only yield a bandit foe;
Then spring upon the caitiffs, steel in hand,
  And strike the fated blow.

AUGUSTUS JULIAN REQUIER
(*Alabama*)

"A REBEL SOLDIER KILLED IN THE TRENCHES BEFORE PETERSBURG, VA., APRIL 15, 1865."

Killed in the trenches! How cold and bare
  The inscription graved on the white card there.
'Tis a photograph, taken last Spring, they say,
  Ere the smoke of battle had cleared away—
Of a rebel soldier—just as he fell,
When his heart was pierced by a Union shell;
And his image was stamped by the sunbeam's ray,
As he lay in the trenches that April day.

Oh God! Oh God! How my woman's heart
  Thrills with a quick, convulsive pain,
As I view, unrolled by the magic of Art,
  One dreadful scene from the battle-plain:—
White as the foam of the storm-tossed wave,
Lone as the rocks those billows lave—
Gray sky above—cold clay beneath—
A gallant form lies stretched in death!

With his calm face fresh on the trampled clay,
  And the brave hands clasped o'er the manly breast:
Save the sanguine stains on his jacket gray,
  We might deem him taking a soldier's rest.
Ah no! Too red is that crimson tide—
Too deeply pierced that wounded side;
Youth, hope, love, glory—manhood's pride—
Have all in vain Death's bolt defied.

His faithful carbine lies useless there,
  As it dropped from its master's nerveless ward;
And the sunbeams glance on his waving hair
  Which the fallen cap has ceased to guard—
Oh Heaven! spread o'er it thy merciful shield,

No more to my sight be the battle revealed!
Oh fiercer than tempest—grim Hades as dread—
On woman's eye flashes the field of the dead!

The scene is changed: In a quiet room,
  Far from the spot where the lone corpse lies,
A mother kneels in the evening gloom
  To offer her nightly sacrifice,
The noon is past, and the day is done,
She knows that the battle is lost or won—
Who lives? Who died? Hush! be thou still!
The boy lies dead on the trench-barred hill.

A KENTUCKY GIRL

"LET ME KISS HIM FOR HIS MOTHER"

Let me kiss him for his mother,
  Let me kiss his dear, youthful brow;
I will love him for his mother,
  And seek her blessing now.
Kind friends have soothed his pillow,
  Have watched his every care,
Beneath the weeping willow,
  O lay him gently there.

CHORUS

Sleep, dearest, sleep;
  I loved you as a brother,
Kind friends around you weep;
  I've kissed you for your mother.

Let me kiss him for his mother;
  What though left a lone stranger here;
She has loved him as none other;
  I feel her blessing near.

Though cold that form lies sleeping,
  Sweet angels watch around.
Dear friends are near thee weeping;
  O, lay him gently down.

CHORUS

Let me kiss him for his mother;
  Or, perchance, fond sister dear.
If a father or a brother,
  I know their blessing's here.
Then kiss him for his mother;
  'Twill soothe her after years.
Farewell, dear stranger, brother;
  Our requiem, our tears.

CHORUS

AUTHOR UNKNOWN

MELT THE BELLS

Melt the bells, melt the bells,
  Still the tinkling on the plains,
And transmute the evening chimes
Into war's resounding rhymes,
  That the invaders may be slain
    By the bells.

Melt the bells, melt the bells,
  That for years have called to prayer,
And, instead, the cannon's roar
Shall resound the valleys o'er,
  That the foe may catch despair
    From the bells.

Melt the bells, melt the bells,
  Though it cost a tear to part
With the music they have made,
Where the friends we love are laid,
  With pale cheek and silent heart,
    'Neath the bells.

Melt the bells, melt the bells,
  Into cannon, vast and grim,
And the foe shall feel the ire
From each heaving lungs of fire,
  And we'll put our trust in Him
    And the bells.

Melt the bells, melt the bells,
  And when foes no more attack,
And the lightning cloud of war
Shall roll thunderless and far,
  We will melt the cannon back
    Into bells.

Melt the bells, melt the bells,
And they'll peal a sweeter chime,
And remind of all the brave
Who have sunk to glory's grave,
  And will sleep thro' coming time
    'Neath the bells.

F. V. Rockett

(*Memphis Appeal*)

SEA-WEEDS

Friend of the thoughtful mind and gentle heart!
  Beneath the citron-tree—
Deep calling to my soul's profunder deep—
  I hear the Mexique Sea.

While through the night rides in the spectral surf
  Along the spectral sands,
And all the air vibrates, as if from harps
  Touched by phantasmal hands.

Bright in the moon the red pomegranate flowers
  Lean to the Yucca's bells,
While with her chrism of dew, sad Midnight fills
  The milk-white asphodels.

Watching all night—as I have done before—
  I count the stars that set,
Each writing on my soul some memory deep
  Of Pleasure or Regret;

Till, wild with heart-break, toward the East I turn,
  Waiting for dawn of day;—
And chanting sea, and asphodel and star
  Are faded, all, away.

Only within my trembling, trembling hands—
  Brought unto me by thee—
I clasp these beautiful and fragile things,
  Bright sea-weeds from the sea,

Fair bloom the flowers beneath these Northern skies,
  Pure shine the stars by night,
And grandly sing the grand Atlantic waves
  In thunder-throated might;

But, as the sea-shell in her chambers keeps
  The murmur of the sea,
So the deep-echoing memories of my home
  Will not depart from me.

Prone on the page they lie, these gentle things!
  As I have seen them cast
Like a drowned woman's hair, along the beach,
  When storms were over-past;

Prone, like mine own affections, cast ashore
  In Battle's storm and blight;
Would they had died, like sea-weeds! Pray forgive me,
  But I must weep tonight.

Tell me again, of Summer fields made fair
  By Spring's precursing plough;
Of joyful reapers, gathering tear-sown harvests—
  Talk to me,—will you—now!

ANNIE CHAMBERS KETCHUM

A BALLAD OF EMMA SAMSON

The courage of man is one thing, but that of a maid is more,
For blood is blood, and death is death, and grim is the battle gore,
And the rose that blooms, tho' blistered by the sleet of an open sky,
Is fairer than its sisters are
Who sleep in the hothouse nigh.

Word came up to Forrest that Streight was on a raid—
Two thousand booted bayonets were riding down the glade.
Eight thousand were before him—he was holding Dodge at bay,
But he turned on his heels like the twist of a steel,
And was off at the break of day.

* * *

A fight to the death in the valley, and a fight to the death on the
  hill,
But still Streight thunder'd southward, and Forrest followed still.
And the goaded hollows bellow'd to the bay of the rebel gun—
For Forrest was hot as a solid shot
When its fight is just begun.

* * *

A midnight fight on the mountain, and a daybreak fight in the glen,
And when Streight stopped for water he had lost three hundred men.
But he gained the bridge at the river and planted his batteries there,
And the halt of the gray was a hound at bay,
And the blue—a wolf in his lair.

And out from the bridge at the river a white heat lightning came,
Like the hungry tongues of a forest fire, with the autumn woods aflame;
And the death-smoke burst above them, and the death-heat blazed below,
But the men in gray cheered the smoke away,
And bared their breast to the blow.

"To the ford! To the ford!" rang the bugle—"and flank the enemy out!"
And quick to the right the gray lines wheel and answer with a shout.
But the river was mad and swollen—to left—to right—no ford—
And still the sting of the maddened thing
At the bridge, and still the goad.

Then out from a nearby cabin a mountain maiden came,
Her cheeks were banks of snowdrifts, but her eyes were skies of flame,
And she drew her sunbonnet closer as the bullets whispered low—
(Lovers of lead), and one of them said:
"I'll clip a curl as I go!"

Straight through the blistering bullets she fled like a hunted doe,
While the hound-guns down at the river bayed in her wake below.

And around, their hot breath shifted, and behind, their pattering feet,
But still she fled through the thunder red,
And still through the lightning sleet.

And she stood at the General's stirrup, flushed as a mountain rose,
When the sun looks down in the morning, and the gray mist upward goes.
She stood at the General's stirrup and this was all she said:
"I'll lead the way to the ford today—
I'm a girl; but I'm not afraid!"

How the gray troops thronged around her! And then the rebel yell—
With that brave girl to lead them they would storm the gates of hell!
And they toss her behind the General, and again the echoes woke,
For she clung to him there with her floating hair
As the wild vine clings to the oak.

Down through the bullets she led them, down through an unused road,
And, when the General dismounted to use his glass on the ford,
She spread her skirts before him (the troopers gave a cheer):
"Better get behind me, General,
For the bullets will hit you here!"

And then the balls came singing and ringing quick and hot,
But the gray troops gave them ball for ball and answer shot for shot.
"They have riddled your skirt," the General said, "I must take you out of this din."
"Oh, that's all right," she answered light—
"They are wounding my crinoline!"

And then, in a blaze of beauty, her sunbonnet off she took,
Right in the front she waved it high and at their lines it shook.
And the gallant bluecoats cheered her—ceased firing to a man,
And the graycoats rode through the bloody ford,
And again the race began.

JOHN TROTWOOD MOORE
(*Tennessee*)

"LORENA"

(*A Popular Camp Song of the Civil War*)

The years creep slowly by, Lorena;
The snow is on the grass again;
The sun's low down the sky, Lorena;
The frost gleams where the flowers have been.
But the heart throbs on as warmly now
As when the summer days were nigh;
Oh! the sun can never dip so low
Adown affection's cloudless sky.

A hundred months have passed, Lorena,
Since last I held that hand in mine,
And felt the pulse beat fast, Lorena,
Though mine beat faster far than thine,
A hundred months—'twas flowery May,
When up the hilly slope we climbed,
To watch the dying of the day
And hear the distant church bells chimed.

We loved each other then, Lorena,
More than we ever dared to tell;
And what we might have been, Lorena,
Had but our loving prospered well!
But then, 'tis past; the years have gone,
I'll not call up their shadowy forms;
I'll say to them, Lost years sleep on,
Sleep on, nor heed life's pelting storms.

The story of the past, Lorena,
  Alas! I care not to repeat;
The hopes that could not last, Lorena,
  They lived, but only lived to cheat.
I would not cause e'en one regret
  To rankle in your bosom now—
"For if we try we may forget,"
  Were words of thine long years ago.

Yes, these were words of thine, Lorena—
  They are within my memory yet—
They touched some tender chords, Lorena,
  Which thrill and tremble with regret.
'Twas not the woman's heart which spoke—
  Thy heart was always true to me;
A duty stern and piercing broke
  The tie which linked my soul with thee.

It matters little now, Lorena,
  The past is in the eternal past;
Our hearts will soon lie low, Lorena,
  Life's tide is ebbing out so fast.
There is a future, oh, thank God!
  Of life this is so small a part—
'Tis dust to dust beneath the sod,
  But there, up there, 'tis heart to heart.

J. P. Webster

JOHN PELHAM

Just as the spring came laughing through the strife
  With all its gorgeous cheer;
In the bright April of historic life
  Fell the great cannoneer.

The wondrous lulling of a hero's breath
  His bleeding country weeps—

Hushed in the alabaster arms of death,
  Our young Marcellus sleeps.

Nobler and grander than the Child of Rome,
  Curbing his chariot steeds;
The knightly scion of a Southern home
  Dazzled the land with deeds.

Gentlest and bravest in the battle brunt,
  The champion of the truth,
He bore his banner to the very front
  Of our immortal youth.

A clang of sabres 'mid Virginian snow,
  The fiery pag of shells—
And there's a wail of immemorial woe
  In Alabama dells.

The pennon drops that led the sacred band
  Along the crimson field!
The meteor blade sinks from the nerveless hand
  Over the spotless shield.

We gazed and gazed upon that beauteous face,
  While 'round the lips and eyes,
Couched in the marble slumber, flashed the grace
  Of a divine surprise.

Oh, mother of a blessed soul on high!
  Thy tears may soon be shed—
Think of thy boy with princes of the sky,
  Among the Southern dead.

How must he smile on this dull world beneath,
  Fevered with swift renown—
He—with the martyr's amaranthine wreath
  Twining the victor's crown!

JAMES R. RANDALL

GENERAL DABNEY H. MAURY

He sleeps, the "little general" sleeps,
  With all the great before him;
Another son Virginia weeps,
  Proud that 'twas she who bore him.

Away from home, far, far away,
  He crossed life's utmost barrier;
Subdued, but still without dismay
  He comes, our gentle warrior.

He fell not, 'twas his cause that fell,
  Upon the field of glory.
He lived, that living he might tell
  His country's gallant story.

With heroes he was wont to share
  The trial and the peril;
With them to do, with them to dare,
  With them shall be his burial.

He rests, the tired soldier rests,
  Upon the field of battle,
Recalling deeds of dauntless breasts
  And scenes of boyish prattle.

He sleeps, the "little General" sleeps,
  With all the great before him;
Virginia now her vigil keeps,
  Proud that 'twas she who bore him.

ROSEWELL PAGE

ULRIC DAHLGREN

(*March 2, 1864*)

A flash of light across the night,
  An eager face, and eye afire!
O lad so true, you yet may rue
  The courage of your deep desire!

"Nay tempt me not; the way is plain—
'T is but the coward checks his rein;
  For there they lie,
  And there they cry,
For whose dear sake 't were joy to die!"

He bends unto his saddlebow,
  The steeds they follow two and two;
Their flanks are wet with foam and sweat,
  Their riders' locks are damp with dew.

"O comrades, haste! the way is long,
The dirge it drowns the battle-song;
  The hunger preys,
  The famine slays,
An awful horror veils our ways!"

Beneath the pall of prison wall
  The rush of hoofs they seem to hear;
From loathsome guise they lift their eyes,
  And beat their bars and bend their ear.

"Ah, God be thanked! our friends are nigh;
He wills it not that thus we die;
  O fiends accurst
  O Want and Thirst,
Our comrades gather,—do your worst!"

A sharp affright runs through the night,
  An ambush stirred, a column reined;
The hurrying steed has checked his speed,
  His smoking flanks are crimson stained.

O noble son of noble sire,
Thine ears are deaf to our desire!
    O knightly grace
    Of valiant race,
The grave is honor's trysting-place!

O life so pure! O faith so sure!
  O heart so brave, and true, and strong!
With tips of flame is writ your name,
  In annaled deed and storied song!

It flares across the solemn night,
It glitters in the radiant light;
    A jewel set,
    Unnumbered yet,
In our Republic's coronet!

KATE BROWNLEE SHERWOOD

THE STAR-SPANGLED BANNER

Oh, say, can you see, by the dawn's early light,
What so proudly we hailed at the twilight's last gleaming—
Whose broad stripes and bright stars, through the perilous fight,
O'er the ramparts we watched were so gallantly streaming!
And the rocket's red glare, the bombs bursting in air,
Gave proof through the night that our flag was still there;
Oh, say, does that star-spangled banner yet wave
O'er the land of the free and the home of the brave?

On the shore dimly seen through the mists of the deep,
  Where the foe's haughty host in dread silence reposes,
What is that which the breeze, o'er the towering steep,
  As it fitfully blows, now conceals, now discloses?
Now it catches the gleam of the morning's first beam,
In full glory reflected now shines on the stream;
'Tis the star-spangled banner; oh, long may it wave
O'er the land of the free and the home of the brave!

And where is that band who so vauntingly swore
  That the havoc of war and the battle's confusion
A home and a country should leave us no more?
  Their blood has washed out their foul footsteps' pollution.
No refuge could save the hireling and slave
From the terror of flight, or the gloom of the grave;
And the star-spangled banner in triumph doth wave
O'er the land of the free and the home of the brave!

Oh, thus be it ever, when freemen shall stand
  Between their loved homes and the war's desolation!
Blest with victory and peace, may the heav'n-rescued land
  Praise the power that hath made and preserved us a nation.
Then conquer we must, when our cause it is just,
And this be our motto—"IN GOD IS OUR TRUST:"
And the star-spangled banner in triumph shall wave
O'er the land of the free, and the home of the brave.

FRANCIS SCOTT KEY

THE CONFEDERACY

Born in a day, full-grown our Nation stood,
  The pearly light of heaven was on her face
Life's early joy was coursing in her blood;
  A thing she was of beauty and of grace.

She stood, a stranger on the great broad earth,
  No voice of sympathy was heard to greet
The glory-beaming morning of her birth,
  Or hail the coming of the unsoiled feet.

She stood, derided by her passing foes;
  Her heart beat calmly 'neath their look of scorn:
Their rage in blackening billows round her rose—
  Her brow, meanwhile, as radiant as the morn.

Their poisonous coils about her limbs are cast,
  She shakes them off in pure and holy ire,
As quietly as Paul, in ages past,
  Shook off the serpent in the crackling fire.

She bends not to her foes, nor to the world,
  She bears a heart for glory, or for gloom;
But with her starry cross, her flag unfurled,
  She kneels amid the sweet magnolia bloom.

She kneels to Thee, O God, she claims her birth,
  She lifts to Thee her young and trusting eye,
She asks of Thee her place upon the earth—
  For it is Thine to give or to deny.

Oh, let Thine eye but recognize her right!
  Oh, let Thy voice but justify her claim!
Like grasshoppers are nations in Thy sight,
  And all their power is but an empty name.

Then listen, Father, listen to her prayer!
  Her robes are dripping with her children blood;
Her foes around "like bulls of Bashan stare,"
  They fain would sweep her off, "as with a flood."

The anguish wraps her close around, like death,
  Her children lie in heaps about her slain;
Before the world she bravely holds her breath,
  Nor gives one utterance to a note of pain.

But 'tis not like Thee to forget the oppressed,
  Thou feel'st within her heart the stifled moan—
Thou Christ! Thou Lamb of God! oh, give her rest!
  For thou hast called her!—is she not Thine own?

JANE T. H. CROSS

"THE BALTIMORE GRAYS"

Ah, well I remember that long summer's day
When, round about Richmond our broken ranks lay.
Week in and week out they had been at the front,
And bore without flinching the battle's fierce brunt.
Till, shattered and weary, we needed repose
Ere we met in death-struggle our numberless foes.
Our knapsacks were empty, our uniforms worn,
Our feet, from long marching, were naked and torn;
But not a man grumbled in the rank or the file,
We bore all our hardships with a joke and a smile,
For Jackson was with us, and under his eye,
Each soldier determined to do or to die.

That evening old Jack had us out to review,
When a glance down the line showed us all something new—
Eighty-seven young boys from old Baltimore,
Who had run the blockade and that day joined the corps.
Their clothes were resplendent, all new, spick and span—
'Twas plain that a tailor had measured each man.
When we learned who they were what a shout we did raise!
How we cheered our new allies, the "Baltimore Grays!"

There were Lightfoots and Carters, and Howards and Kanes,
The grandsons of Carroll, the nephews of Gaines,
And in each of the brave boys dressed up in a row,
You could see the pure blood of the proud Huguenot.

But we were old vets of Stonewall's brigade;
We'd been fighting so long that war seemed a trade;
And some of us laughed at the youngsters so gay
Who had come to the battle as if coming to play;
And all through the camp you could hear the rough wits
Cry, "Hullo, young roosters!" and "Dandified cits!"
But the boys took it bravely, and heartily laughed
At the hungry "Confeds" by whom they were chaffed,
Till one ragged soldier, more bold than the rest,
Fired off this rough joke, which we all thought the best:
"Boys, you'd better go home; 'tis getting quite late."
Then the girlish-faced captain spoke up and said, "Wait!"

They didn't wait long, for the very next day
We were ordered right off to the thick of the fray;
For early that morning we'd heard the dull roar
Of the guns of our foeman on Rapidan's shore,
And all of us knew, with old Jack in command,
If fighting was near him, he'd at once take a hand.
And, sure enough, soon marching orders we got,
And we swung down the road in "foot-cavalry" trot.
The boys were behind us. I fell to the rear,
To see how the youngsters on march would appear.
Their files were close up, their marching was true,
I reported to Stonewall, "Yes, General, they'll do."

In a few minutes more the action began.
We met the first shock, for we were the van;
But we stood to our ranks like oaks of the field,
For Stonewall's brigade never knew how to yield.
Upon us, however, a battery played,

And huge gaps in our ranks were now and then made,
Till Jackson commanded a charge up the hill.
We charged—in a moment the cannon were still.
Jackson said to the Grays, "Such valor you've shown,
You'll veterans be ere your beards are full grown;
In this, your first action, you've proved yourself bold;
I'll station you here, these guns you must hold."

Then the girlish-faced captain, so straight and so tall,
Saluted, and said, "You'll here find us all,
For, wherever stationed, this company stays."
How we laughed, how we cheered the bold Baltimore Grays!
But the red tide of battle around us still flowed,
And we followed our leader, as onward he rode;
Cried "Good-by" to the boys; "take care of the guns—
We'll relieve you as soon as the enemy runs."
Ah, yes, indeed! soon the brave boys were relieved,
But not in the manner we all had believed;
Alas, the sisters who weep and the mothers who pine
For the loved and the lost of the Maryland line!

By some fatal blunder our left was exposed,
And by thousands of Federals the boys were enclosed;
They asked for no quarter, their Maryland blood
Never dreamed of surrender, they fell where they stood.
We heard in the distance the firing and noise,
And double-quicked back to the help of the boys.
The guns were soon ours; but oh, what a sight!
Every Baltimore boy had been killed in the fight,
Save the girlish-faced captain, and he scarce alive.
When he saw us around him he seemed to revive,
And smiled when we told him the field had been won,
And the Baltimore Grays had saved every gun.

The Stonewall rode up and endeavored to speak,
But his utterance was choked, and down his bronzed cheek

The hot tears flowed, as he gazed on the dead,
"God pity their mothers and sisters!" he said.
Then, dismounting, he knelt on the blood-sodden sand,
And prayed while he held the dying boy's hand;
The gallant young hero said, "General, I knew
That the Grays to your orders would always be true;
You'll miss not a Gray from our final call;
Look around you, my General—you'll here find us all."
The blood gushed from his mouth, his head sunk on his breast,
And the girlish-faced captain lay dead with the rest.

AUTHOR UNKNOWN

SONG OF OUR GLORIOUS SOUTHLAND

Oh, sing of our glorious Southland,
The pride of the golden sun!
'Tis the fairest land of flowers
The eye e'er looked upon.

Sing of her orange and myrtle
That glitter like gems above;
Sing of her dark-eyed maidens
As fair as a dream of love.

Sing of her flowing rivers—
How musical their sound!
Sing of her dark green forests,
The Indian hunting-ground.

Sing of the noble nation
Fierce struggling to be free;
Sing of the brave who barter
Their lives for liberty!

Weep for the maid and matron
  Who mourn their loved ones slain;
Sigh for the light departed,
  Never to shine again:

'Tis the voice of Rachel weeping,
  That never will comfort know;
'Tis the wail of desolation,
  The breaking of hearts in woe!

Ah! the blood of Abel crieth
  For vengeance from the sod!
'Tis a brother's hand that's lifted
  In the face of an angry God!

Oh! brother of the Northland,
  We plead from our father's grave;
We strike for our homes and altars,
  He fought to build and save!

A smouldering fire is burning,
  The Southern heart is steeled—
Perhaps 'twill break in dying,
  But never will it yield.

MRS. MARY WARE

THE COUNTERSIGN

Alas! the rolling hours pass slow—
  The night is very dark and still—
And in the marshes far below
  Is heard the lonely whippoorwill;
I scarce can see a foot ahead—
  My ears are strained to catch each sound,
I feel the dead leaves beneath me spread
  And the springs bubbling thro' the ground.

Along the beaten path I pace,
  Where white rays mark my sentry's track;
In formless things I seem to trace;
  The foeman's form, with bended back.
I think I see him crouching low!
  I stop and list—I stop and peer—
Until the neighboring hillocks grow
  To groups of soldiers, far and near.

With ready piece I wait and watch
  Until my eyes familiar grown—
Detect each harmless earthen notch,
  And turn "guerrillas" into stone;
And then amid the lonely gloom,
  Beneath tall magnolia trees,
My silent marches I resume
  And think of other times than these.

"Halt! who goes there?" my challenge cry—
  It rings along the watchful lone—
"Relief!" I hear a voice reply.
  "Advance and give the countersign!"
With bayonet at the charge I wait—
  The corporal gives the mystic spell—
With "arms aport" I charge my mate
  Then onward pass, and all is well!

But in my tent, that night awake,
  I ask, "if in the fray I fall,
Can I the mystic answer make
  When the angelic sentries call?"
And pray that Heaven so ordain,
  Where'er I go, what fate be mine,
Whether in pleasure or in pain
  I still may have the "countersign!"

Author Unknown

"WOULDST THOU HAVE ME LOVE THEE?"

Wouldst thou have me love thee, dearest!
  With a woman's proudest heart,
Which shall ever hold thee nearest,
  Shrined in its inmost part?
Listen, then! My country's calling
  On her sons to meet the foe!
Leave these groves of rose and myrtle;
  Drop thy dreamy harp of love!
Like young Korner—scorn the turtle,
  When the eagle screams above!

Dost thou pause?—Let dastards dally—
  Do thou for thy country fight!
'Neath her noble emblem rally—
  "God, our country, and our right!"
Listen! now her trumpet's calling
  On her sons to meet the foe!
Woman's heart is soft and tender,
  But 'tis proud and faithful, too;
Shall she be her land's defender?
  Lover! Soldier! up and do!

Seize thy father's ancient falchion,
  Which once flashed as freedom's star!
Till sweet peace—the bow and halcyon,
  Stilled the stormy strife of war.
Listen! now their country's calling
  On her sons to meet her foe!
Sweet is love in moonlight bowers!
  Sweet the altar and the flame!
Sweet the spring-time with her flowers!
  Sweeter far the patriot's name!

Should the God who smiles above thee,
  Doom thee to a soldier's grave,
Hearts will break, but fame will love thee,
  Canonized among the brave!
Listen, then! thy country's calling
  On her sons to meet the foe!
Rather would I view thee lying
  On the last red field of strife,
'Mid thy country's heroes dying,
  Than become a dastard's wife!

ALEXANDER B. MEEK

O, TEMPORA! O, MORES!

"Great Pan is dead!" so cried an airy tongue
  To one who, drifting down Calabria's shore,
Heard the last knell, in starry midnight rung,
  Of the old Oracles, dumb for evermore.

A low wail ran along the shuddering deep,
  And as, far off, its flaming accents died,
The awe-struck sailors, startled from their sleep,
  Gazed, called aloud: no answering voice replied;

Nor ever will—the angry Gods have fled,
  Closed are the temples, mute are all the shrines,
The fires are quenched, Dodona's growth is dead,
  The Sibyl's leaves are scattered to the winds.

No mystic sentence will they bear again,
  Which, sagely spelled, might ward a nation's doom;
But we have left us still some god-like men,
  And some great voices pleading from the tomb.

If we would heed them, they might save us yet,
  Call up some gleams of manhood in our breasts,
Truth, valor, justice, teach us to forget
  In a grand cause our selfish interests.

But we have fallen on evil times indeed,
  When public faith is but the common shame,
And private morals held an idiot's creed,
  And old-world honesty an empty name.

And lust, and greed, and gain are all our arts!
  The simple lessons which our fathers taught
Are scorned and jeered at; in our sordid marts
  We sell the faith for which they toiled and fought.

Each jostling each in the mad strife for gold,
  The weaker trampled by the reckless throng
Friends, honor, country lost, betrayed or sold,
  And lying blasphemies on every tongue.

Cant for religion, sounding words for truth,
  Fraud leads to fortune, gelt for guilt atones,
No care for hoary age or tender youth,
  For widows' tears or helpless orphans' groans,

The people rage, and work their own wild will,
  They stone the prophets, drag their highest down,
And as they smite, with savage folly still
  Smile at their work, those dead eyes wear no frown.

The sage of "Drainfield" tills a barren soil,
  And reaps no harvest where he sowed the seed,
He has but exile for long years of toil;
  Nor voice in council, though his children bleed.

And never more shall "Redcliff's" oaks rejoice,
  Now bowed with grief above their master's bier;
Faction and party stilled that mighty voice,
  Which yet could teach us wisdom, could we hear.

And "Woodland's" harp is mute; the gray, old man
  Broods by his lonely hearth and weaves no song;
Or, if he sing, the note is sad and wan,
  Like the pale face of one who's suffered long.

So all earth's teachers have been overborne
  By the coarse crowd, and fainting droop or die;
They bear the cross, their bleeding brows the thorn,
  And ever hear the clamor—"Crucify!"

Oh, for a man with godlike heart and brain!
  A god in stature, with a god's great will,
And fitted to the time, that not in vain
  Be all the blood we've spilt and yet must spill.

Oh, brothers! friends! shake off the Circean spell!
  Rouse to the dangers of impending fate!
Grasp your keen swords, and all may yet be well—
  More gain, more pelf, and it will be, too late!

John Dickson Burns, M.D.

(*Charleston Mercury, 1864*)

"WHEN THIS CRUEL WAR IS OVER"

Dearest one, do you remember
  When we last did meet;
When you told me how you loved me
  Kneeling at my feet?
Oh! how proud you stood before me
  In your suit of gray,
When you vowed for me and country
  Ne'er to go astray.

CHORUS

Weeping sad and lonely
  Sighs and tears how vain,
When this cruel war is over,
  Pray that we meet again.

When the summer breeze is sighing
  Mournfully along,
Or when autumn leaves are falling,
  Sadly breathes the song.
Oft in dreams I see you lying
  On the battle plain,
Lonely, wounded, even dying,
  Calling, but in vain.

CHORUS

If amid the din of battle
  Nobly you should fall,
Far away from those who love you—
  None to hear you call—
Who would whisper words of comfort?
  Who would soothe your pain?
Ah, the many cruel fancies
  Ever in my brain!

CHORUS

But our country called you, loved one—
  Angels guide your way;
While our "Southern boys" are fighting,
  We can only pray.
When you strike for God and freedom,
  Let all nations see
How you love our Southern Banner—
  Emblem of the free.

CHORUS

HENRY TUCKER

THE TWO ARMIES

Two armies stand enrolled beneath
The banner with the starry wreath;
One, facing battle, blight and blast,
Through twice a hundred fields has passed;
Its deeds against a ruffian foe,
Stream, valley, hill, and mountain know,
Till every wind that sweeps the land
Goes, glory-laden, from the strand.

The other, with a narrower scope,
Yet led by not less grand a hope,
Hath won, perhaps, as proud a place,
And wears its fame with meeker grace.
Wives march beneath its glittering sign,
Fond mothers swell the lovely line;
And many a sweetheart hides her blush
In the young patriot's generous flush.

No breeze of battle ever fanned
The colors of that tender band;
Its office is beside the bed,
Where throbs some sick or wounded head.
It does not court the soldier's tomb,
But plies the needle and the loom;
And, by a thousand peaceful deeds,
Supplies a struggling nation's needs.

Nor is that army's gentle night
Unfelt amid the deadly fight;
It nerves the son's, the husband's hand,
It points the lover's fearless brand;
It thrills the languid, warms the cold,
Gives even new courage to the bold.
And sometimes lifts the veriest clod
To its own lofty trust in God.

When Heaven shall blow the trump of peace,
And bid this weary warfare cease,
Their several missions nobly done,
The triumph grasped, and freedom won,
Both armies, from their toils at rest,
Alike may claim the victor's crest,
But each shall see its dearest prize
Gleam softly from the other's eyes.

HENRY TIMROD

"DEAR MOTHER, I'VE COME HOME TO DIE"

Dear mother, I remember well
The parting kiss you gave me,
When merry rang the village bell—
My heart was full of joy and glee;
I did not dream that one short year
Would crush the hopes that soared so high!
Oh, mother dear, draw near to me;
Dear mother, I've come home to die.

CHORUS

Call sister, brother, to my side,
And take your soldier's last good-by,
Oh, mother dear, draw near to me!
Dear mother, I've come home to die.

Hark! mother, 'tis the village bell;
I can no longer with thee stay;
My country calls, to arms! to arms!
The foe advances in fierce array!
The vision's past—I feel that now
For country I can only sigh.
Oh, mother dear, draw near to me!
Dear mother! I've come home to die.

Dear mother, sister, brother, all,
One parting kiss—to all good-by:
Weep not, but clasp your hand in mine,
And let me like a soldier die!
I've met the foe upon the field,
Where hosts contending scorned to fly;
I fought for right—God bless you all!—
Dear mother, I've come home to die.

E. Bowers

THE TREE, THE SERPENT, AND THE STAR

From the silver sands of a gleaming shore,
Where the wild sea-waves were breaking,
A lofty shoot from a twining root
Sprang forth as the dawn was waking;
And the crest, though fed by the sultry beam,
(And the shaft by the salt wave only)
Spread green to the breeze of the curling seas,
And rose like a column lonely.
Then hail to the tree, the Palmetto tree,
Ensign of the noble, the brave, and the free.

As the sea-winds rustled the bladed crest,
And the sun to the noon rose higher
A serpent came, with an eye of flame,
And coiled by the leafy pyre;
His ward he would keep by the lonely tree,
To guard it with constant devotion;
Oh, sharp was the fang, and the armed clang,
That pierced through the roar of the ocean,
And guarded the tree, the Palmetto tree,
Ensign of the noble, the brave, and the free.

And the day wore down to the twilight close,
The breeze died away from the billow;

Yet the wakeful clang of the rattles rang
  Anon from the serpent's pillow;
When I saw through the night a gleaming star
  O'er the branching summit growing,
Till the foliage green and the serpent's sheen
  In the golden light were glowing,
    That hung o'er the tree, the Palmetto tree
    Ensign of the noble, the brave and the free.

By the standard cleave every loyal son,
  When the drums' long roar shall rattle;
Let the folds stream high to the victor's eye
    Or sink in the shock of the battle.
Should triumph rest on the red field won,
  With a victor's song let us hail it;
If the battle fail and the star grow pale,
  Yet never in shame will we veil it,
    But cherish the tree, the Palmetto tree,
    Ensign of the noble, the brave, and the free.

A. P. Gray
(*South Carolina*)

BEYOND THE POTOMAC

(*September 7, 1862*)

They slept on the field which their valor had won,
But arose with the first early blush of the sun,
For they knew that a great deed remained to be done,
  When they passed o'er the river.

They arose with the sun, and caught life from his light,—
Those giants of courage, those Anaks in fight,—
And they laughed out aloud in the joy of their might,
  Marching swift for the river.

On! on! like the rushing of storms through the hills;
On! on! with a tramp that is firm as their wills;
And the one heart of thousands grows buoyant, and thrills,
  At the thought of the river.

Oh, the sheen of their swords! the fierce gleam of their eyes!
It seemed as on earth a new sunlight would rise,
And, king-like, flash up to the sun in the skies,
  O'er their path to the river.

But their banners, shot-scarred, and all darkened with gore,
On a strong wind of morning streamed wildly before,
Like the wings of death-angels swept fast to the shore,
  The green shore of the river.

As they march, from the hillside, the hamlet, the stream,
Gaunt throngs whom the foemen had manacled, teem,
Like men just aroused from some terrible dream,
  To cross sternly the river.

They behold the broad banners, blood-darkened, yet fair,
And a moment dissolves the last spell of despair,
While a peal, as of victory, swells on the air,
  Rolling out to the river.

And that cry, with a thousand strange echoings, spread,
Till the ashes of heroes were thrilled in their bed,
And the deep voice of passion surged up from the dead,
  "Ay, press on to the river!"

On! on! like the rushing of storms through the hills,
On! on! with a tramp that is firm as their wills,
And the one heart of thousands grows buoyant, and thrills,
  As they pause by the river.

Then the wan face of Maryland, haggard and worn,
At this sight lost the touch of its aspect forlorn,
And she turned on the foemen, full-statured in scorn,
  Pointing stern to the river.

And Potomac flowed calmly, scarce heaving her breast,
With her low-lying billows all bright in the west,
For a charm as from God lulled the waters to rest
  Of the fair rolling river.

Passed! passed! the glad thousands march safe through the tide;
Hark, foeman, and hear the deep knell of your pride,
Ringing weird-like and wild, pealing up from the side
  Of the calm-flowing river!

'Neath a blow swift and mighty the tyrant may fall:
Vain! vain! to his gods swells a desolate call;
Hath his grave not been hollowed, and woven his pall,
  Since they passed o'er the river?

PAUL HAMILTON HAYNE
(*South Carolina*)

"IN HIS BLANKET ON THE GROUND"

Weary, weary lies the soldier,
  In his blanket on the ground
With no sweet "Good-night" to cheer him,
  And no tender voice's sound,
Making music in the darkness,
  Making light his toilsome hours,
Like a sunbeam in the forest,
  Or a tomb wreathed o'er with flowers.

Thoughtful, hushed, he lies, and tearful,
  As his memories sadly roam
To the "cozy little parlor"
  And the loved ones of his home;
And his waking and his dreaming
  Softly braid themselves in one,
As the twilight is the mingling
  Of the starlight and the sun.

And when sleep descends upon him,
  Still his thought within his dream
Is of home, and friends, and loved ones,
  And his busy fancies seem
To be real, as they wander
  To his mother's cherished form.

As she gently said, in parting,
  "Thine in sunshine and in storm:
Thine in helpless childhood's morning,
  And in boyhood's joyous time,
Thou must leave me now—God watch thee
  In thy manhood's ripened prime."

Or, mayhap, amid the phantoms
  Teeming thick within his brain,
His dear father's locks, o'er-silvered,
  Come to greet his view again;
And he hears his trembling accents,
  Like a clarion ringing high,
"Since not mine are youth and strength, boy,
  Thou must victor prove, or die."

Or perchance he hears whisper
  Of the faintest, faintest sigh,
Something deeper than word-spoken,
  Something breathing of a tie
Near his soul as bounding heart-blood:
  It is hers, that patient wife—
And again that parting seemeth
  Like the taking leave of life:

And her last kiss he remembers,
  And the agonizing thrill,
And the "Must you go?" and answer,
  "I but know my Country's will."

Or the little children gather,
  Half in wonder, round his knees;
And the faithful dog, mute, watchful,
  In the mystic glass he sees;
And the voice of song, and pictures,
  And the simplest homestead flowers,
Unforgotten, crowd before him
  In the solemn midnight hours.

Then his thoughts in Dreamland wander
  To a sister's sweet caress,
And he feels her dear lips quiver
  As his own they foundly press;
And he hears her proudly saying,
  (Though sad tears are in her eyes),
"Brave men fall, but live in story,
  For the Hero never dies!"

Or, perhaps, his brown cheek flushes,
  And his heart beats quicker now,
As he thinks of one who gave him
  Him, the loved one, love's sweet vow;
And, ah, fondly he remembers
  He is still her dearest care,
Even in his star-watched slumber
  That she pleads for him in prayer.

Oh, the soldier will be dreaming,
  Dreaming often of us all,
(When the damp earth is his pillow,
  And the snow and cold sleet fall),
Of the dear, familiar faces,
  Of the cozy, curtained room,
Of the flitting of the shadows
  In the twilight's pensive gloom.

Or when summer suns burn o'er him,
  Bringing drought and dread disease,
And the throes of wasting fever
  Come his weary frame to seize—
In the restless sleep of sickness,
  Doomed, perchance, to martyr death,
Hear him whisper "Home," sweet cadence,
  With his quickened, labored breath.

Then God bless him, bless the soldier,
  And God nerve him for the fight;
May He lend his arm new prowess
  To do battle for the right.
Let him feel that while he's dreaming
  In his fitful slumber bound,
That we're praying—God watch o'er him
  In his blanket on the ground.

CAROLINE H. GERVAIS
(*South Carolina*)

THE VIRGINIANS OF THE VALLEY

The knightliest of the knightly race
  That, since the days of old,
Have kept the lamp of chivalry
  Alight in hearts of gold:
The kindliest of the kindly band
  That, rarely hating ease,
Yet rode with Spotswood round the land,
  And Raleigh round the seas;

Who climbed the blue Virginian hills
  Against embattled foes,
And planted there, in valleys fair,
  The lily and the rose;

Whose fragrance lives in many lands,
  Whose beauty stars the earth,
And lights the hearths of happy homes
  With loveliness and worth.

We thought they slept!—the sons who kept
  The names of noble sires,
And slumbered while the darkness crept
  Around their vigil-fires;
But aye the "Golden Horseshoe" knights
  Their old Dominion keep,
Whose foes have found enchanted ground,
  But not a knight asleep!

FRANCIS ORRERY TICKNOR

"I GIVE MY SOLDIER BOY A BLADE"

I give my soldier boy a blade,
  In fair Damascus fashioned well:
Who first the glittering falchion swayed,
  Who first beneath its fury fell,
I know not; but I hope to know,
  That, for no mean or hireling trade,
To guard no feeling base or low—
  I give my soldier boy the blade!

Cool, calm and clear—the lucid flood
  In which its tempering work was done;—
As calm, as clear, in wind and wood,
  Be thou where'er it sees the sun!
For country's claim, at honor's call,
  For outraged friend, insulted maid,
At mercy's voice to bid it fall—
  I give my soldier boy the blade!

The eye which marked its peerless edge,
  The hand that weighed its balanced poise,
Anvil and pincers, forge and wedge,
  Are gone, with all their flame and noise;
Yet still the gleaming sword remains!
  So, when in dust I low am laid,
Remember, by these heart-felt strains,
  I give my soldier boy the blade!

H. M. L.

CLEBURNE

Another ray of light hath fled, another Southern brave
Hath fallen in his country's cause and found a laureled grave—
Hath fallen, but his deathless name shall live when stars shall set,
For, noble Cleburne, thou art one this world will ne'er forget.

'Tis true, thy warm heart beats no more, that on thy noble head
Azrael placed his icy hand, and thou art with the dead;
The glancing of thine eyes are dim; no more will they be bright
Until they ope in Paradise, with clearer, heavenlier light.

No battle news disturbs thy rest upon the sun-bright shore,
No clarion voice awakens thee on earth to wrestle more,
No tramping steed, no wary foe bids thee awake, arise,
For thou art in the angel world, beyond the starry skies.

Brave Cleburne, dream in thy low bed, with pulseless deadened
    heart;
Calm, calm and sweet, O warrior rest! thou well hast borne thy
    part,
And now a glory wreath for thee the angels singing twine,
A glory wreath, not of the earth, but made by hands divine.

A long farewell—we give thee up, with all thy bright renown,
A chieftain here on earth is lost, in heaven an angel found.
Above thy grave a wail is heard—a nation mourns her dead;
A nobler for the South ne'er died, a braver never bled.

A last farewell—how can we speak the bitter word farewell!
The anguish of our bleeding hearts vain words may never tell.
Sleep on, sleep on, to God we give our chieftain in his might;
And weeping, feel he lives on high, where comes no sorrow's night.

AUTHOR UNKNOWN

(*Selma Despatch, 1864*)

OUR DEPARTED COMRADES

I am sitting alone by a fire
  That glimmers on Sugar Loaf's height,
But before I to rest shall retire
  And put out the fast-fading light—
While the lanterns of heaven are ling'ring
  In silence all o'er the deep sea,
And loved ones at home are yet mingling
  Their voices in converse of me—
While yet the lone seabird is flying
  So swiftly far o'er the rough wave,
And many fond mothers are sighing
  For the noble, the true, and the brave;
Let me muse o'er the many departed
  Who slumber on mountain and vale;
With the sadness which shrouds the lone-hearted,
  Let me tell of my comrades a tale.

Far away in the green, lonely mountains,
  Where the eagle makes bloody his beak,
In the mist, and by Gettysburg's fountains,
  Our fallen companions now sleep!

Near Charleston, where Sumter still rises
  In grandeur above the still wave,
And always at evening discloses
  The fact that her inmates yet live—
On islands, and fronting Savannah,
Where dark oaks o'ershadow the ground,
Round Macon and smoking Atlanta,
  How many dead heroes are found!
And out on the dark swelling ocean,
  Where vessels go, riding the waves,
How many, for love and devotion,
  Now slumber in warriors' graves!

No memorials have yet been erected
  To mark where these warriors lie,
All alone, save by angels protected,
  They sleep 'neath the sea and the sky!
But think not that they are forgotten,
  By those who the carnage survive:
When their headboards will all have grown rotten,
  And the night-winds have levelled their graves,
Then hundreds of sisters and mothers,
  Whose freedom they perished to save,
And fathers, and empty-sleeved brothers,
  Who surmounted the battle's red wave;
Will crowd from their homes in the Southward,
  In search of the loved and the blest,
And, rejoicing, will soon return homeward
    And lay our dear martyrs to rest.

J. Marion Shirer

SWING LOW, SWEET CHARIOT

(*Slave Song*)

I looked over Jordan and what did I see
  Coming for to carry me home?
A band of angels coming after me,
  Coming for to carry mc home.

CHORUS

Swing low, sweet chariot
Coming for to carry me home,
Swing low, sweet chariot
Coming for to carry me home.

If you get there before I do,
  Coming for to carry me home
Tell all my friends I'm coming too
  Coming for to carry me home.

The brightest day that ever I saw,
  Coming for to carry me home,
When Jesus washed my sins away,
  Coming for to carry me home.

I'm sometimes up and sometimes down,
  Coming for to carry me home.
But still my soul feels heavenly bound,
  Coming for to carry me home.

NO LAND LIKE OURS

Though other lands may boast of skies
  Far deeper in their blue,
Where flowers in Eden's pristine dyes,
  Bloom with a richer hue;
And other nations pride in kings,
  And worship lordly powers;
Yet every voice of nature sings,
  There is no land like ours.

Though other scenes than such as grace
  Our forests, fields, and plains,
May lend the earth a sweeter face
  Where peace incessant reigns;
But dearest still to me the land
  Where sunshine cheers the hours,
For God hath shown, with His own hand,
  There is no land like ours!

Though other streams may softer flow
  In vales of classic bloom,
And rivers clear as crystal glow,
  That wear no tinge of gloom;
Though other mountains lofty look,
  And grand seem olden towers,
We see, as in an open book,
  There is no land like ours!

Though other nations boast of deeds
  That live in old renown,
And other peoples cling to creeds
  That coldly on us frown;
On pure religion, love, and law
  Are based our ruling powers—
The world but feels, with wondering awe,
  There is no land like ours!

Though other lands may boast their brave,
  Whose deeds are writ in fame,
Their heroes ne'er such glory gave
  As gilds our country's name;
Though others rush to daring deeds,
  Where the darkening war-cloud lowers,
Here, each alike for freedom bleeds—
  There is no land like ours!

Though other lands Napoleon
  And Wellington adorn,
America, her Washington,
  And later heroes born;
Yet Johnston, Jackson, Price, and Lee,
  Bragg, Buckner, Morgan towers,
With Beauregard, and Hood, and Bee—
  There is no land like ours!

J. R. Barrick
(*Kentucky*)

A BATTLE BALLAD

To General J. E. Johnston

A summer Sunday morning,
  July the twenty-first,
In eighteen hundred sixty-one,
  The storm of battle burst.

For many a year the thunder
  Had muttered deep and low,
And many a year, through hope and fear,
  The storm had gathered slow.

Now hope had fled the hopeful,
  And fear was with the past;
And on Manassas' cornfields
  The tempest broke at last.

A wreath above the pine-tops,
  The booming of a gun;
A ripple on the cornfields,
  And battle was begun.

A feint upon our centre,
  While the foeman massed his might,
For our swift and sure destruction,
  With his overwhelming "right."

All the summer air was darkened
  With the tramping of their host;
All the Sunday stillness broken
  By the clamor of their boast.

With their lips of savage shouting,
  And their eyes of sullen wrath,
Goliath, with the weaver-beam,
  The champion of Gath.

Are they men who guard the passes,
  On our "left" so far away?
In the cornfields, O Manassas!
  Are they men who fought to-day?

Our boys are brave and gentle,
  And their brows are smooth and white;
Have grown to men, Manassas,
  In the watches of a night?

Beyond the grassy hillocks
  There are tents that glimmer white;
Beneath the leafy covert
  There is steel that glistens bright.

There are eyes of watchful reapers
  Beneath the summer leaves,
With a glitter as of sickles
  Impatient for the sheaves.

They are men who guard the passes,
  They are men who bar the ford;
Stands our David at Manassas,
  The champion of the Lord.

They are men who guard our altars,
  And beware ye sons of Gath,
The deep and dreadful silence
  Of the lion in your path.

Lo! the foe was mad for slaughter,
  And the whirlwind hurtled on;
But our boys had grown to heroes,
  They were lions every one.

And they stood a wall of iron,
  And they shone a wall of flame,
And they beat the baffled tempest
  To the caverns whence it came.

And Manassas' sun descended
  On their armies crushed and torn,
On a battle bravely ended,
  On a nation grandly born.

The laurel and the cypress,
  The glory and the grave,
We pledge to thee, O Liberty!
  The life-blood of the brave.

FRANCIS ORRERY TICKNOR

THE BIVOUAC OF THE DEAD

The muffled drum's sad roll has beat
  The soldier's last tattoo;
No more on life's parade shall meet
  That brave and fallen few.
On Fame's eternal camping-ground
  Their silent tents are spread,
And Glory guards, with solemn round,
  The bivouac of the dead.

No rumor of the foe's advance
  Now swells upon the wind;
No troubled thought at midnight hours
  Of loved ones left behind;
No vision of the morrow's strife
  The warrior's dream alarms;
No braying horn nor screaming fife
  At dawn shall call to arms.

Their shivered swords are red with rust,
  Their plumed heads are bowed;
Their haughty banner, trailed in dust,
  Is now their martial shroud.
And plenteous funeral tears have washed
  The red stains from each brow,
And the proud forms, by battle gashed,
  Are free from anguish now.

The neighing troop, the flashing blade,
  The bugle's stirring blast,
The charge, the dreadful cannonade,
  The din and shout, are past;
Nor war's wild note nor glory's peal
  Shall thrill with fierce delight
Those breasts that never more may feel
  The rapture of the fight.

Full many a norther's breath has swept
  O'er Angostura's plain,—
  And long the pitying sky has swept
  Above its mouldered slain.
The raven's scream, or eagle's flight,
  Or shepherd's pensive lay,
Alone awakes each sullen height
  That frowned o'er that dread fray.

Sons of the Dark and Bloody Ground,
  Ye must not slumber there,
Where stranger steps and tongues resound
  Along the heedless air.
Your own proud land's heroic soil
  Shall be your fitter grave:
She claims from war his richest spoil—
  The ashes of her brave.

Thus 'neath their parent turf they rest,
  Far from the gory field,
Borne to a Spartan mother's breast
  On many a bloody shield;
The sunshine of their native sky
  Smiles sadly on them, here,
And kindred eyes and hearts watch by
  The heroes' sepulchre.

Rest on, embalmed and sainted dead!
  Dear as the blood ye gave;
No impious footstep here shall tread
  The herbage of your grave;
Nor shall your glory be forgot
  While Fame her record keeps,
Or Honor points the hallowed spot
  Where Valor proudly sleeps.

Yon marble minstrel's voiceless stone
  In deathless song shall tell
Where many a vanished age hath flown,
  The story how ye fell;
Nor wreck, nor change, nor winter's blight,
  Nor Time's remorseless doom,
Shall dim one ray of glory's light
  That gilds your deathless tomb.

THEODORE O'HARA
(*Kentucky*)

UNDER THE SHADE OF THE TREES

What are the thoughts that are stirring his breast?
  What is the mystical vision he sees?
—"Let us pass over the river, and rest
  Under the shade of the trees."

Has he grown sick of his toils and his tasks?
  Sighs the worn spirit for respite or ease?
Is it a moment's cool halt that he asks
  "Under the shade of the trees."

Is it the gurgle of waters whose flow
  Ofttime has come to him, borne on the breeze,
Memory listens to, lapsing so low,
  Under the shade of the trees?

Nay—though the rasp of the flesh was so sore,
  Faith, that had yearnings far keener than these,
Saw the soft sheen of the Thitherward Shore
  Under the shade of the trees;—

Caught the high psalms of ecstatic delight—
  Heard the harps harping, like soundings of seas—
Watched earth's assoiled ones walking in white
  Under the shade of the trees.

Oh, was it strange he should pine for release,
  Touched to the soul with such transports as these,—
He who so needed the balsam of peace,
  Under the shade of the trees?

Yea, it was noblest for him—it was best
  (Questioning naught of our Father's decrees),
There to pass over the river and rest
  Under the shade of the trees!

MARGARET JUNKIN PRESTON

BOWING HER HEAD

Her head is bowed downwards; so pensive her air,
As she looks on the ground with her pale solemn face,
It were hard to decide whether faith or despair,
Whether anguish or trust, in her heart holds a place.

Her hair was all gold in the sun's joyous light,
Her brow was as smooth as the soft, placid sea;
But the furrows of care came with shadows of night,
And the gold silvered pale when the light left the lea.

Her lips slightly parted, deep thought in her eye,
While sorrow cut seams in her forehead so fair:
Her bosom heaves gently, she stifles a sigh,
And just moistens her lid with the dews of a tear.

Why droops she thus earthward—why bends she? Oh, see!
There are gyves on her limbs! see her manacled hand!
She is loaded with chains; but her spirit is free—
Free to love and to mourn for her desolate land.

Her jailer, though cunning, lacks wit to devise
How to fetter her thoughts, as her limbs he has done;
The eagle that's snatched from his flight to the skies,
From the bars of his cage may still gaze at the sun.

No sound does she utter; all voiceless her pains;
The wounds of her spirit with pride she conceals;
She is dumb to her shearers; the clank of her chains
And the throbs of her heart only tell what she feels.

She looks sadly around her; how sombre the scene!
How thick the deep shadows that darken her view!
The black embers of homes where the earth was so green,
And the smokes of her wreck where the heavens shone blue.

Her daughters bereaved of all succor but God,
Her bravest sons perished—the light of her eyes;
But oppression's sharp heel does not cut 'neath the sod,
And she knows that the chains cannot bind in the skies.

She thinks of the vessel she aided to build,
Of all argosies richest that floated the seas;
Compacted so strong, framed by architects skilled
Or to dare the wild storm, or to sail to the breeze,

To balmiest winds blowing soft where she steers,
The favor of Heaven illuming her path—
She might sail as she pleased in the mild summer airs,
And avoid the dread regions of tempest and wrath.

But the crew quarreled soon o'er the cargo she bore;
'Twas adjusted unfairly, the cavillers said;
And the anger of men marred the peace that of yore
Spread a broad path of glory and sunshine ahead.

There were seams in her planks—there were spots on her flag—
So the fanatics said, as they seized on her helm;
And from soft summer seas, turned her prow where the crag
And the wild breakers rose the good ship to o'erwhelm.

Then the South, though true love to the vessel she bore,
Since she first laid its keel in the days that were gone—
Saw it plunge madly on to the wild billow's roar,
And rush to destruction and ruin forlorn.

So she passed from the decks, in the faith of her heart
That Justice and God her protectors would be;
Not dashed like a frail, fragile spar, without chart,
In the fury and foam of the wild raging sea.

The life-boat that hung by the stout vessel's side
  She seized and embarked on the wide, trackless main,
In the faith that she'd reach, making virtue her guide,
  The haven the mother-ship failed to attain.

But the crew rose in wrath, and they swore by their might
  They would sink the brave boat that did buffet the sea,
For daring to seek, by her honor and right,
  A new port from the storms, a new home for the free.

So they crushed the brave boat; all forbearance they lost;
  They littered with ruins the ocean so wild—
Till the hulk of the parent ship, beaten and tossed,
  Drifted prone on the flood by the wreck of the child.

And the bold rower, loaded with fetters and chains,
  In the gloom of her heart sings the proud vessel's dirge;
Half forgets, in its wreck, all the pangs of her pains,
  As she sees its stout parts floating loose in the surge.

AUTHOR UNKNOWN

(*Savannah Broadside*)

THE DEATH OF LYON

(*August 10, 1861*)

Sing bird, on green Missouri's plain,
  The saddest song of sorrow;
Drop tears, O clouds, in gentlest rain
  Ye from the winds can borrow;
Breathe out, ye winds, your softest sigh,
  Weep, flowers, in dewy splendor,
For him who knew well how to die,
  But never to surrender.

Up rose serene the August sun
  Upon that day of glory;
Up curled from musket and from gun
  The war-cloud, gray and hoary;
It gathered like a funeral pall,
  Now broken, and now blended,
Where rang the bugle's angry call,
  And rank with rank contended.

Four thousand men, as brave and true
  As e'er went forth in daring,
Upon the foe that morning threw
  The strength of their despairing.
They feared not death—men bless the field
  That patriot soldiers die on;
Fair Freedom's cause was sword and shield,
  And at their head was Lyon.

Their leader's troubled soul looked forth
  From eyes of troubled brightness;
Sad soul! the burden of the North
  Had pressed out all its lightness.
He gazed upon the unequal fight,
  His ranks all rent and gory.
And felt the shadows close like night
  Round his career of glory.

"General, come lead us!" loud the cry
  From a brave band was ringing—
"Lead us, and we will stop, or die,
  That battery's awful singing!"
He spurred to where his heroes stood—
  Twice wounded, no one knowing—
The fire of battle in his blood
  And on his forehead glowing.

Oh! cursed for aye that traitor's hand,
  And cursed that aim so deadly,
Which smote the bravest of the land,
  And dyed his bosom redly.
Serene he lay, while past him pressed
  The battle's furious billow,
As calmly as a babe may rest
  Upon its mother's pillow.

So Lyon died: and well may flowers
  His place of burial cover,
For never had this land of ours
  A more devoted lover.
Living, his country was his bride;
  His life he gave her, dying;
Life, fortune, love, he nought denied
  To her, and to her sighing.

Rest, patriot, in thy hillside grave,
  Beside her form who bore thee!
Long may the land thou diedst to save
  Her bannered stars wave o'er thee!
Upon her history's brightest page,
  And on fame's glowing portal,
She'll write thy grand, heroic age,
  And grave thy name immortal.

HENRY PETERSON

(*Missouri*)

A GEORGIA VOLUNTEER

Far up the lonely mountain-side
  My wandering footsteps led;
The moss lay thick beneath my feet,
  The pine sighed overhead.
The trace of a dismantled fort
  Lay in the forest nave,
And in the shadow near my path
  I saw a soldier's grave.

The bramble wrestled with the weed
  Upon the lowly mound,
The simple headboard, rudely writ,
  Had rotted to the ground;
I raised it with a reverent hand,
  From dust its words to clear,
But time had blotted all but these—
  "A Georgia Volunteer."

I saw the toad and scaly snake
  From tangled covert start,
And hide themselves among the weeds
  Above the dead man's heart;
But undisturbed, in sleep profound,
  Unheeding, there he lay;
His coffin but the mountain soil,
  His shroud Confederate gray.

I heard the Shenandoah roll
  Along the vale below,
I saw the Alleghanies rise
  Towards the realms of snow.
The "Valley Campaign" rose to mind,—
  Its leader's name—and then
I knew the sleeper had been one
  Of Stonewall Jackson's men.

Yet whence he came, what lip shall say?
  Whose tongue will ever tell
What desolated hearths and hearts
  Have been because he fell?
What sad-eyed maiden braids her hair,
  Her hair which he held dear?
One lock of which, perchance, lies with
  The Georgia Volunteer!

What mother, with long watching eyes
  And white lips cold and dumb,
Waits with appalling patience for
  Her darling boy to come?
Her boy! whose mountain grave swells up
  But one of many a scar
Out in the face of our fair land
  By gory-handed war.

What fights he fought, what wounds he wore
  Are all unknown to fame;
Remember, on his lonely grave
  There is not e'en a name!
That he fought well and bravely, too,
  And held his country dear,
We know, or else he had never been
  A Georgia Volunteer.

He sleeps—what need to question now
  If he were wrong or right?
He knows ere this whose cause was just
  In God the Father's sight.
He wields no warlike weapons now,
  Returns no foeman's thrust,—
Who but a coward would revile
  An honest soldier's dust?

Roll, Shenandoah, proudly roll,
  Adown thy rocky glen,
Above thee lies the grave of one
  Of Stonewall Jackson's men.
Beneath the cedar and the pine,
  In solitude austere,
Unknown, unnamed, forgotten, lies
  A Georgia Volunteer.

MARY ASHLEY TOWNSEND

THE MEN

In the dusk of the forest shade
  A sallow and dusty group reclined;
  Gallops a horseman up the glade—
    "Where will I your leader find?
Tidings I bring from the morning's scout—
I've borne them o'er mound, and moor, and fen."
"Well, sir, stay not hereabout,
  Here are only a few of 'the men.'

"Here no collar has bar or star,
  No rich lacing adorns a sleeve;
Further on our officers are,
  Let them your report receive.
Higher up, on the hill up there,
  Overlooking this shady glen,
There are their quarters—don't stop here,
  We are only some of 'the men.'

"Yet stay, courier, if you bear
  Tidings that the fight is near;
Tell them we're ready, and that where
  They wish us to be we'll soon appear;
Tell them only to let us know
  Where to form our ranks, and when;
And we'll teach the vaunting foe
  That they've met a few of 'the men.'

"We're the men, though our clothes are worn—
  We're the men, though we wear no lace—
We're the men, who the foe hath torn,
  And scattered their ranks in dire disgrace;
We're the men who have triumphed before—
  We're the men who will triumph again;
For the dust, and the smoke, and the cannon's roar,
  And the clashing bayonets—'we're the men.' "

"Ye who sneer at the battle-scar,
Of garments faded, and soiled and bare,
Yet who have for the 'star and bars'
Praise and homage and dainty fare;
Mock the wearers and pass them on,
Refuse them kindly word—and then
Know, if your freedom is ever won
By human agents—these are the men!

MAURICE BELL

ONLY A PRIVATE

Only a private! his jacket of gray
Is stained by the smoke and the dust;
As Bayard he's brave, as Rupert he's gay,
Reckless as Murat in heat of the fray,
But in God is his only trust!

Only a private! to march and fight,
Suffer and starve and be strong;
With knowledge enough to know that the might
Of justice and truth, and freedom and right
In the end must crush out the wrong!

Only a private! no ribbon or star
Shall gild with false glory his name!
No honors for him in braid or in bar,
His Legion of Honor is only a scar,
And his wounds are his roll of fame!

Only a private! one more hero slain
On the field lies silent and chill!
And in the far South a wife prays in vain—
One clasp of the hands she may ne'er clasp again,
One kiss from the lips that are still!

Only a private! there let him sleep,
He will need no tablet nor stone;
For the mosses and vines o'er his grave will creep,
And at night the stars through the clouds will peep
And watch him who lies there alone!

Only a martyr! who fought and who fell,
Unknown and unmarked in the strife;
But still as he lies in his lonely cell,
Angel and seraph the legend shall tell—
Such a death is eternal life

F. W. D.

OUR DEAD HEROES

The angels above us hover,
And the breezes a requiem sing,
As we meet this day to cover,
Our dead with the flowers of Spring.
They were brave, they were true, devoted,
They died for their country's laws,
And Montgomery will e'er be noted
As the cradle of their cause.

The waves of the Alabama
Will no longer be seen to roll,
Ere the men of that mighty drama
Shall fade from memory's scroll.
The names of Lee and Davis
Shall gild the wing of time,
Their armies and their navies,
Be praised for deeds sublime!

Since then long years have vanished,
Their forms have gone to dust,
Their flags have all been banished,
Their swords have gone to rust.

But their souls are up in glory,
And now like angels gleam;
Last night their mystic story,
Came to me in a dream.

MORTON BRYAN WHARTON, D.D.

OUR CHRISTMAS HYMN

"Good-will and peace! peace and good-will!"
The burden of the Advent song,
What time the love-charmed waves grew still
To hearken to the shining throng;
The wondering shepherds heard the strain
Who watched by night the slumbering fleece,
The deep skies echoed the refrain,
"Peace and good-will, good-will and peace!"

And wise men hailed the promised sign,
And brought their birth-gifts from the East,
Dear to that Mother as the wine
That hallowed Cana's bridal feast;
But what to these are myrrh or gold,
And what Arabia's costliest gem,
Whose eyes the Child divine behold,
The blessed Babe of Bethlehem.

"Peace and good-will, good-will and peace!"
They sing, the bright ones overhead;
And scarce the jubilant anthems cease
Ere Judah wails her first-born dead;
And Rama's wild, despairing cry
Fills with great dread the shuddering coast,
And Rachel hath but one reply,
"Bring back, bring back my loved and lost."

So, down two thousand years of doom
  That cry is borne on wailing winds,
But never star breaks through the gloom
  No cradled peace the watcher finds;
And still the Herodian steel is driven,
  And breaking hearts make ceaseless moan,
And still the mute appeal to Heaven
  Man answers back with groan for groan.

How shall we keep our Christmas tide?
  With that dread past, its wounds agape,
Forever walking by our side,
  A fearful shade, an awful shape;
Can any promise of the spring
  Make green the faded autumn leaf?
Or who shall say that time will bring
  Fair fruit to him who sows but grief?

Wild bells! that shake the midnight air
  With those dear tones that custom loves,
You wake no sounds of laughter here,
  Nor mirth in all our silent groves;
On one broad waste, by hill or flood,
  Of ravaged lands your music falls,
And where the happy homestead stood
  The stars look down on roofless halls.

At every board a vacant chair
  Fills with quick tears some tender eye,
And at our maddest sports appear
  Those well-loved forms that will not die.
We lift the glass, our hand is stayed—
  We jest, a spectre rises up—
And weeping, though no word is said,
  We kiss and pass the silent cup.

And pledge the gallant friend who keeps
  His Christmas-eve on Malvern's height,
And him, our fair-haired boy, who sleeps
  Beneath Virginian snows to-night;
While, by the fire, she, musing, broods
  On all that was and might have been,
If Shiloh's dank and oozing woods
  Had never drunk that crimson stain.

O happy Yules of buried years!
  Could ye but come in wonted guise,
Sweet as love's earliest kiss appears,
  When looking back through wistful eyes,
Would seem those chimes whose voices tell
  His birth-night with melodious burst,
Who, sitting by Samaria's well,
  Quenched the lorn widow's life-long thirst.

Ah! yet I trust that all who weep,
  Somewhere, at last, will surely find
His rest, if through dark ways they keep
  The child-like faith, the prayerful mind:
And some far Christmas morn shall bring
  From human ills a sweet release
To loving hearts, while angels sing
  "Peace and good-will, good-will and peace!"

John Dickson Burns, M.D.
(*South Carolina*)

TO A DEJECTED FRIEND

What though thy way is often dark,
  And billows loudly round thee roar,
Be firm, droop not; thy gallant bark
  Unharmed shall reach the destined shore.

There's much in life that's left thee still;
The good outweighs the evil here;
The less thou dwell'st upon the ill
The more will happiness appear.

For all there gleams a promise sure;
Who thinks his lot in misery cast
Should patient wait, in faith endure,
The blessing rich will come at last.

And be not overmuch concerned
When passions wild thy peace annoy;
I've long ago this lesson learned,
"No gold's without its base alloy."

Should Slander's voice around thee ring,
Pass on, stoop not to make reply;
Thus pluck the venom from the sting,
And leave the crawling worm to die.

Thy virtues, like the rock-bound coast
That guards us from the treacherous main,
Will dash the waves by Envy tossed
Back on the powerless flood again.

MORTON BRYAN WHARTON, D.D.

OUR CONFEDERATE DEAD

Unknown to me, brave boy, but still I wreathe
For you the tenderest of wildwood flowers;
And o'er your tomb a virgin's prayer I breathe,
To greet the pure moon and the April showers.

I only know, I only care to know,
You died for me—for me and country bled;
A thousand Springs and wild December snow
Will weep for one of all the Southern dead.

Perhaps some mother gazes up the skies,
  Wailing like Rachel, for her martyred brave—
Oh, for her darling sake, my dewy eyes
  Moisten the turf above your lowly grave.

The cause is sacred, when our maidens stand
  Linked with sad matrons and heroic sires,
Above the relics of a vanquished land
  And light the torch of sanctifying fire.

Your bed of honor has a rosy cope
  To shimmer back the tributary stars;
And every petal glistens with a hope
  Where Love hath blossomed in the disk of Mars.

Sleep! on your couch of glory slumber comes
  Bosomed amid the archangelic choir;
Not with the grumble of impetuous drums
  Deep'ning the chorus of embattled ire.

Above you shall the oak and cedar fling
  Their giant plumage and protecting shade;
For you the song-bird pause upon his wing
  And warble requiems ever undismayed.

Farewell! And if your spirit wander near
  To kiss this plant of unaspiring art—
Translate it, even in the heavenly sphere,
  As the libretto of a maiden's heart.

H. M. WHARTON, D.D.

STACK ARMS

"Stack Arms!" I've gladly heard the cry
  When, weary with the dusty tread
Of marching troops, as night drew nigh,
  I sank upon my soldier bed,

And calmly slept; the starry dome
  Of heaven's blue arch my canopy,
And mingled with my dreams of home,
  The thoughts of Peace and Liberty.

"Stack Arms!" I've heard it, when the shout
  Exulting, rang along our line,
Of foes hurled back in bloody rout,
  Captured, dispersed; its tones divine
Then came to mine enraptured ear.
  Guerdon of duty nobly done,
And glistening on my cheek the tear
  Of grateful joy for victory won.

"Stack Arms!" In faltering accents, slow
  And sad, it creeps from tongue to tongue.
A broken, murmuring wail of woe,
  From manly hearts by anguish wrung,
Like victims of a midnight dream,
  We move, we know not how nor why,
For life and hope but phantoms seem,
  And it would be relief—to die!

JOSEPH BLYTH ALSTON

ON THE HEIGHTS OF MISSION RIDGE

When the foes, in conflict heated,
  Battled over road and bridge,
While Bragg sullenly retreated
  From the heights of Mission Ridge,—
There, amid the pines and wildwood,
  Two opposing colonels fell,
Who had schoolmates been in childhood,
  And had loved each other well.

There, amid the roar and rattle,
  Facing Havoc's fiery breath,
Met the wounded two in battle,
  In the agonies of death.
But they saw each other reeling
  On the dead and dying men,
And the old time, full of feeling,
  Came upon them once again.

When that night the moon came creeping,
  With its gold streaks, o'er the slain,
She beheld two soldiers, sleeping,
  Free from every earthly pain.
Close beside the mountain heather,
  Where the rocks obscure the sand,
They had died, it seems, together,
  As they clasped each other's hand.

J. AUGUSTINE SIGNAIGO

THE EMPTY SLEEVE

Tom, old fellow, I grieve to see
  The sleeve hanging loose at your side;
The arm you lost was worth to me
  Every Yankee that ever died,
But you don't mind it at all,
  You swear you've a beautiful stump,
And laugh at that damnable ball—
  Tom, I knew you were always a trump.

A good right arm, a nervy hand,
  A wrist as strong as a sapling oak,
Buried deep in the Malvern sand—
  To laugh at that is a sorry joke.
Never again your iron grip
  Shall I feel in my shrinking palm—
Tom, Tom, I see your trembling lip;
  All within is not calm.

Well! the arm is gone, it is true;
  But the one that is nearest the heart
Is left—and that's as good as two;
  Tom, old fellow, what makes you start?
Why, man, she thinks that empty sleeve
  A badge of honor; so do I,
And all of us—I do believe
  The fellow is going to cry!

"She deserves a perfect man," you say;
  "You were not worth her in your prime;"
Tom! the arm that has turned to clay,
  Your whole body has made sublime;
For you have placed in the Malvern earth
  The proof and pledge of a noble life—
And the rest, henceforward of higher worth
    Will be dearer than all to your wife,

I see the people in the street
  Look at your sleeve with kindling eyes;
And you know, Tom, there's naught so sweet
  As homage shown in mute surmise.
Bravely your arm in battle strove,
  Freely for Freedom's sake you gave it;
It has perished—but a nation's love
In proud remembrance will save it.

Go to your sweetheart, then, forthwith—
  You're a fool for staying so long—
Woman's love you'll find no myth,
  But a truth—living, tender, strong.
And when around her slender belt
  Your left is clasped in fond embrace,
Your right will thrill, as if it felt,
  In its grave, the usurper's place.

As I look through the coming years,
  I see a one-armed married man;
A little woman, with smiles and tears,
  Is helping as hard as she can
To put on his coat, to pin his sleeve,
  Tie his cravat, and cut his food;
And I say, as these fancies I weave,
  "That is Tom, and the woman he wooed."

The years roll on, and then I see
  A wedding picture, bright and fair;
I look closer, and it's plain to me
  That is Tom with the silver hair.
He gives away the lovely bride,
  And the guests linger, loth to leave
The house of him in whom they pride—
  "Brave old Tom with the empty sleeve."

Dr. J. R. Bagby
(*Virginia*)

PRO MEMORIA

Lo! the Southland Queen, emerging
  From her sad and wintry gloom,
Robes her torn and bleeding bosom
  In her richest orient bloom.

Chorus—(Repeat first line three times.)

For her weary sons are resting
By the Edenshore;
They have won the crown immortal,
And the cross of death is o'er!
Where the Oriflamme is burning
On the starlit Edenshore!

Brightly still, in gorgeous glory,
God's great jewel lights our sky;
Look! upon the heart's white dial
There's a *shadow* flitting by!

CHORUS—But the weary feet are resting, etc.

Homes are dark and hearts are weary,
Souls are numb with hopeless pain,
Nor the footfall on the threshold
Never more to sound again!

CHORUS—They have gone from us forever,
Aye, for evermore!
We must win the crown immortal,
Follow where they led before,
Where the Oriflamme is burning
On the starlit Edenshore.

Proudly, as our Southern forests
Meet the winter's shafts so keen;
Time-defying memories cluster
Round our hearts in living green.

CHORUS—They have gone from us forever, etc.

May our faltering voices mingle
In the angel-chanted psalm;
May our earthly chaplets linger
By the bright celestial palm.

CHORUS—They have gone from us forever, etc.

When the May eternal dawneth
At the living God's behest,
We will quaff divine Nepenthe,
We will share the Soldier's rest

CHORUS—Where the weary feet are resting, etc.

Where the shadows are uplifted
  'Neath the never-waning sun,
Shout we, Gloria in Excelsis!
  We have lost, but ye have won!

CHORUS—Our hearts are yours forever,
    Aye, for evermore!
    Ye have won the crown immortal,
    And the cross of death is o'er,
    Where the Oriflamme is burning
    On the starlit Edenshore!

INA M. PORTER
(*Indiana*)

READING THE LIST

"Is there any news of the war?" she said.
  "Only a list of the wounded and dead,"
    Was the man's reply
    Without lifting his eye
    To the face of the woman standing by.
" 'Tis the very thing I want," she said;
"Read me a list of the wounded and dead."
He read the list; 'twas a sad array
Of the wounded and killed in the fatal fray.

In the very midst was a pause to tell
Of a gallant youth who fought so well
That his comrades asked: "Who is he, pray?"
"The only son of the Widow Gray,"
    Was the proud reply
    Of his captain nigh....

What ails the woman standing near?
Her face has the ashen hue of fear;
"Well, well, read on; is he wounded? Quick!
O God! but my heart is sorrow-sick!
  Is he wounded?" "No; he fell, they say,
  Killed outright on that fatal day!"
  But see, the woman has swooned away!
Sadly she opened her eyes to the light;
Slowly recalled the events of the fight;
Faintly, she murmured: "Killed outright!
  It has cost me the life of my only son;
  But the battle is fought, and the victory won,
  The will of the Lord, let it be done!"
God pity the cheerless Widow Gray,
And send from the halls of eternal day
The light of His peace to illumine her way.

AUTHOR UNKNOWN

LEE'S PAROLE

"Well, General Grant, have you heard the news?
  How the orders are issued and ready to send
For Lee, and the men in his staff-command,
  To be under arrest,—now the war's at an end?"

"How so? Arrested for what?" he said.
  "Oh, for trial as traitors, to be shot, or hung."
The chief's eye flashed with a sudden ire,
  And his face grew crimson as up he sprung.
"Orderly, fetch me my horse," he said.
  Then into the saddle and up the street,
As if the battle were raging ahead,
  Went the crash of the old war-charger's feet.

"What is this I am told about Lee's arrest,—
Is it true?"—and the keen eyes searched his soul.
"It is true, and the order will be enforced!"
"My word was given in their parole
At Richmond, and that parole
Has not been broken,—nor has my word,
Nor will be until there is better cause
For breaking than this I have lately heard."

"Do you know, sir, whom you have thus addressed?
I am the War Department's head—"
"And I—am General Grant!
At your peril order arrests!" he said.

* * *

A friend is a friend, as we reckon worth,
Who will throw the gauntlet in friendship's fight;
But a man is a man in peace or war
Who will stake his all for an enemy's right.

'Twas a hard-fought battle, but quickly won,—
As a fight must be when 't is soul to soul,—
And 't was years ago; but that honored word
Preserved the North in the South's parole.

MARION MANVILLE

JOHN PEGRAM

What shall we say, now, of our gentle knight,
Or how express the measure of our woe,
For him who rode the foremost in the fight,
Whose good blade flashed so far amid the foe?

Of all his knightly deeds what need to tell?—
That good blade now lies fast within its sheath;
What can we do but point to where he fell,
And, like a soldier, met a soldier's death?

We sorrow not as those who have no hope;
For he was pure in heart as brave in deed—
God pardon us, if blindly we should grope,
And love be questioned by the hearts that bleed.

And yet—oh! foolish and of little faith!
We cannot choose but weep our useless tears;
We loved him so; we never dreamed that death
Would dare to touch him in his brave young years.

Ah dear, browned face, so fearless and so bright!
As kind to friend as thou wast stern to foe—
No more we'll see thee radiant in the fight,
The eager eyes—the flush on cheek and brow!

No more we'll greet the lithe, familiar form,
Amid the surging smoke, with deaf'ning cheer;
No more shall soar above the iron storm,
Thy ringing voice in accents sweet and clear.

Aye! he has fought the fight and passed away—
Our grand young leader smitten in the strife!
So swift to seize the chances of the fray,
And careless only of his noble life.

He is not dead but sleepeth! well we know
The form that lies to-day beneath the sod,
Shall rise that time the golden bugles blow,
And pour their music through the courts of God.

And there amid our great heroic dead—
The war-worn sons of God, whose work is done—
His face shall shine, as they with stately tread,
In grand review, sweep past the jasper throne.

Let not our hearts be troubled, few and brief
His days were here, yet rich in love and faith;
Lord, we believe, help thou our unbelief,
And grant thy servants such a life and death!

W. Gordon McCabe

THE BEAUFORT EXILE'S LAMENT

Now chant me a dirge for the Isles of the Sea,
And sing the sad wanderer's psalm—
Ye women and children in exile that flee
From the land of the orange and palm.

Lament for your homes, for the house of your God,
Now the haunt of the vile and the low;
Lament for the graves of your fathers, now trod
By the foot of the Puritan foe!

No longer for thee, when the sables of night
Are fading like shadows away,
Does the mocking-bird, drinking the first beams of light,
Praise God for the birth of a day.

No longer for thee, when the rays are now full,
Do the oaks form an evergreen glade;
While the drone of the locust o'erhead, seemed to lull
The cattle that rest in the shade.

No longer for thee does the soft-shining moon
Silver o'er the green waves of the bay;
Nor at evening, the notes of the wandering loon
Bid farewell to the sun's dying ray.

Nor when night drops her pall over river and shore,
  And scatters eve's merry-voiced throng,
Does there rise, keeping time to the stroke of the oar,
  The wild chant of the sacred boat-song.

Then the revellers would cease ere the red wine they'd quaff,
  The traveller would pause on his way;
And maidens would hush their low silvery laugh,
  To list to the negro's rude lay.

"Going home! going home!" methinks I now hear
  At the close of each solemn refrain;
'Twill be many a day, aye, and many a year,
  Ere ye'll sing that dear word "Home" again.

Your noble sons slain, on the battle-field lie,
  Your daughters 'mid strangers now roam;
Your aged and helpless in poverty sigh
  O'er the days when they once had a home.

"Going home! going home!" for the exile alone
  Can those words sweep the chords of the soul,
And raise from the grave the loved ones who are gone,
  As the tide-waves of time backward roll.

"Going home! going home!" Ah! how many who pine,
  Dear Beaufort, to press thy green sod,
Ere then will have passed to shores brighter than thine—
  Will have gone home at last to their God!

AUTHOR UNKNOWN

HOSPITAL DUTIES

Fold away all your bright-tinted dresses,
  Turn the key on your jewels today,
And the wealth of your tendril-like tresses
  Braid back in a serious way;
No more delicate gloves, no more laces,
  No more trifling in boudoir or bower,
But come with your souls in your faces
  To meet the stern wants of the hour.

Look around! By the torchlight unsteady
  The dead and the dying seem one—
What! trembling and paling already,
  Before your dear mission's begun?
These wounds are more precious than ghastly—
  Time presses her lips to each scar,
While she chants of that glory which vastly
  Transcends all the horrors of war.

Pause here by this bedside. How mellow
  The light showers down on that brow!
Such a brave, brawny visage, poor fellow!
  Some homestead is missing him now.
Some wife shades her eyes in the clearing,
  Some mother sits moaning distressed,
While the loved one lies faint but unfearing,
  With the enemy's ball in his breast.

Here's another—a lad—a mere stripling,
  Picked up in the field almost dead,
With the blood through his sunny hair rippling
  From the horrible gash in the head.
They say he was first in the action;
  Gay-hearted, quick-headed, and witty:
He fought till he dropped with exhaustion
  At the gates of our fair Southern city.

Fought and fell 'neath the guns of that city,
With a spirit transcending his years—
Lift him up in your large-hearted pity,
And wet his pale lips with your tears.
Touch him gently; most sacred the duty
Of dressing that poor shattered hand!
God spare him to rise in his beauty,
And battle once more for his land!

Pass on! it is useless to linger
While others are calling your care;
There is need for your delicate finger,
For your womanly sympathy there.
There are sick ones athirst for caressing,
There are dying ones raving at home,
There are wounds to be bound with a blessing,
And shrouds to make ready for some.

They have gathered about you the harvest
Of death in its ghastliest view;
The nearest as well as the furthest
Is there with the traitor and true.
And crowned with your beautiful patience,
Made sunny with love at the heart,
You must balsam the wounds of the nations,
Nor falter nor shrink from your part.

And the lips of the mother will bless you,
And angels, sweet-visaged and pale,
And the little ones run to caress you,
And the wives and the sisters cry hail!
But e'en if you drop down unheeded,
What matter? God's ways are the best;
You have poured out your life where 'twas needed,
And He will take care of the rest.

AUTHOR UNKNOWN

THE BALLAD OF CHICKAMAUGA

(*September 19–20, 1863*)

By Chickamauga's crooked stream the martial trumpets blew;
The North and South stood face to face, with War's dread work to do.
O lion-strong, unselfish, brave, twin athletes battle-wise,
Brothers yet enemies, the fire of conflict in their eyes,
All banner-led and bugle-stirred, they set them to the fight,
Hearing the god of slaughter laugh from mountain height to height.

The ruddy, fair-haired, giant North breathed loud and strove amain;
The swarthy shoulders of the South did heave them to the strain;
An earthquake shuddered underfoot, a cloud rolled overhead:
And serpent-tongues of flame cut through and lapped and twinkled red,
Where back and forth a bullet-stream went singing like a breeze,
What time the snarling cannon-balls to splinters tore the trees.

"Make way, make way!" a voice boomed out, "I'm marching to the sea!"
The answer was a rebel yell and Bragg's artillery.
Where Negley struck, the cohorts gray like storm tossed clouds were rent;
Where Buckner charged, a cyclone fell, the blue to tatters went;
The noble Brannan cheered his men, Pat Cleburne answered back,
And Lytle stormed, and life was naught in Walthall's bloody track.

Old Taylor's Ridge rocked to its base, and Pigeon Mountain shook;
And Helm went down, and Lytle died, and broken was McCook.
Van Cleve moved like a hurricane, a tempest blew with Hood,

Awful the sweep of Breckenridge across the flaming wood.
Never before did battle-roar such chords of thunder make,
Never again shall tides of men over such barriers break.

"Stand fast, stand fast!" cried Rosecrans; and Thomas said, "I will!"
And, crash on crash, his batteries dashed their broadsides down the hill.
Brave Longstreet's splendid rush tore through whatever barred its track,
Till the Rock of Chickamauga hurled the roaring columns back,
And gave the tide of victory a red tinge of defeat,
Adding a noble dignity to that hard word, retreat.

Two days they fought, and evermore those days shall stand apart,
Keynotes of epic chivalry within the nation's heart.
Come, come, and set the carven rocks to mark this glorious spot;
Here let the deeds of heroes live, their hatreds be forgot.
Build, build, but never monument of stone shall last as long
As one old soldier's ballad borne on breath of battle-song.

MAURICE THOMPSON

VICKSBURG—A BALLAD

For sixty days and upwards,
A storm of shell and shot
Rained 'round us in a flaming shower,
But still we faltered not!
"If the noble city perish,"
Our brave young leader said,
"Let the only walls the foe shall scale
Be the ramparts of the dead!"

For sixty days and upwards
The eye of heaven waxed dim,
And even throughout God's holy morn,
O'er Christian prayer and hymn,

Arose a hissing tumult,
  As if the fiends of air
Strove to ingulf the voice of faith
  In the shrieks of their despair.

There was wailing in the houses,
  There was trembling on the marts,
While the tempest raged and thundered,
  'Mid the silent thrill of hearts;
But the Lord, our shield, was with us,
  And ere a month had sped
Our very women walked the streets
  With scarce one throb of dread.

And the little children gambolled—
  Their faces purely raised,
Just for a wondering moment,
  As the huge bomb whirled and blazed!
Then turned with silvery laughter
  To the sports which children love,
Thrice mailed in the sweet, instinctive thought,
  That the good God watched above.

Yet the hailing bolts fell faster,
  From scores of flame-clad ships,
And about us, denser, darker,
  Grew the conflict's wild eclipse,
Till a solid cloud closed o'er us,
  Like a type of doom and ire,
Whence shot a thousand quivering tongues
  Of forked and vengeful fire.

But the unseen hands of angels
  Those death-shafts turned aside,
And the dove of heavenly mercy
  Ruled o'er the battle tide;
In the houses ceased the wailing,
  And through the war-scarred marts
The people trod with the step of hope,
  To the music in their hearts.

PAUL H. HAYNE
(*South Carolina*)

A DIRGE FOR McPHERSON

Killed in Front of Atlanta
(*July 22, 1864*)

Arms reversed and banners craped—
  Muffled drums;
Snowy horses sable-draped—
  McPherson comes.
    But, tell us, shall we know him more,
    Lost-Mountain and lone Kenesaw?

Brace the sword upon the pall—
  A gleam in gloom;
So a bright name lighteth all
  McPherson's doom.

Bear him through the chapel-door—
  Let priest in stole
Pace before the warrior
  Who led. Bell—toll!

Lay him down within the nave,
  The Lesson read—
Man is noble, man is brave,
  But man's—a weed.

Take him up again and wend
  Graveward, nor weep:
There's a trumpet that shall rend
  This Soldier's sleep.

Pass the ropes the coffin round,
  And let descend;
Prayer and volley—let it sound
  McPherson's end.
    True fame is his, for life is o'er—
    Sarpedon of the mighty war.

HERMAN MELVILLE

"OH, NO, HE'LL NOT NEED THEM AGAIN"

Oh, no! he'll not need them again—
  No more will he wake to behold
The splendor and fame of his men,
  The tale of his victories told!
No more will he wake from that sleep
  Which he sleeps in his glory and fame,
While his comrades are left here to weep
  Over Cleburne, his grave and his name.

Oh, no! he'll not need them again;
  No more will his banner be spread
O'er the field of his gallantry's fame—
  The soldier's proud spirit is fled!
The soldier who rose 'mid applause,
  From the humblemost place in the van—
I sing not in praise of the cause
  But rather in praise of the man.

Oh, no! he'll not need them again;
  He has fought his last battle without them.
For barefoot he, too, must go in,
  While barefoot stood comrades about him;

And barefoot they proudly marched in,
  With blood flowing fast from their feet;
They thought of the past victories won,
  And the foes that they now were to meet.

Oh, no! he'll not need them again;
  He is leading his men to the charge,
Unheeding the shells, or the slain,
  Or the showers of the bullets at large
On the right, on the left, on the flanks,
  He dashingly pushes his way,
While with cheers, double-quick and in ranks,
  His soldiers all followed that day.

Oh, no! he'll not need them again;
  He falls from his horse to the ground!
Oh, anguish! oh, sorrow! oh, pain!
  In the brave hearts that gathered around.
He breathes not of grief, nor a sigh
  On the breast where he pillowed his head,
Ere he fix'd his last gaze upon high—
  "I'm killed, boys, but fight it out," said.

Oh, no! he'll not need them again;
  But treasure them up for his sake;
And oh! should you sing a refrain
  Of the memories they still must awake,
Sing it soft as the summer-eve breeze,
  Let it sound as refreshing and clear;
Tho' grief-born, there's that which can please
  In thoughts that are gemmed with a tear.

AUTHOR UNKNOWN

CAROLINA

(*April 14, 1861*)

Carolina! Carolina!
  Noble name in State and story,
  How I love thy truthful glory,
  As I love the blue sky o'er ye,
    Carolina evermore!

Carolina! Carolina!
  Land of chivalry unfearing,
  Daughters fair beyond comparing,
  Sons of worth and noble daring,
    Carolina evermore!

Carolina! Carolina!
  Soft thy clasp in loving greeting,
  Plenteous board and kindly meeting,
  All thy pulses nobly beating,
    Carolina evermore!

Carolina! Carolina!
  Green thy valleys, bright thy heaven,
  Bold thy streams through forest riven,
  Bright thy laurels, hero-given,
    Carolina evermore!

Carolina! Carolina!
  Holy name, and dear forever,
  Never shall thy children, never,
  Fail to strike with grand endeavor,
    Carolina evermore!

JOHN A. WAGNER
(*South Carolina*)

THE KNELL SHALL SOUND ONCE MORE

I know that the knell shall sound once more,
  And the dirge be sung o'er a bloody grave,
And there shall be storm on the beaten shore,
  And there shall be strife on the stormy wave;
And we shall wail, with a mighty wail,
  And feel the keen sorrow through many years,
But shall not our banner at last prevail,
  And our eyes be dried of tears?

There's bitter pledge for each fruitful tree,
  And the nation whose course is long to run,
Must make, though in anguish still it be,
  The tribute of many a noble son;
The roots of each mighty shaft must grow
  In the blood-red fountain of many hearts;
And to conquer the right from a bloody foe,
  Brings a pang as when soul and body parts!

But the blood and the pang are the need, alas!
  To strengthen the sovereign will that sways
The generations that rise, and pass
  To the full fruition that crowns their days!
'Tis still in the strife, they must grow to life:
  And sorrow shall strengthen the soul for care;
And the freedom sought must ever be bought
  By the best blood-offerings, held most dear.

Heroes, the noblest, shall still be first
  To mount the red altar of sacrifice;
Homes the most sacred shall fare the worst,
  Ere we conquer and win the precious prize!—
The struggle may last for a thousand years,
  And only with blood shall the field be bought;
But the sons shall inherit, through blood and tears,
  The birthright for which their old fathers fought.

AUTHOR UNKNOWN

ODE RECITED AT THE HARVARD COMMEMORATION

(*July 21, 1865*)

I

Weak-winged is song,
  Nor aims at that clear-ethered height
Whither the brave deed climbs for light:
    We seem to do them wrong,
Bringing our robin's-leaf to deck their hearse
Who in warm life-blood wrote their nobler verse,
Our trivial song to honor those who come
With ears attuned to strenuous trump and drum,
And shaped in squadron-strophes their desire,
Live battle-odes whose lines were steel and fire:
    Yet sometimes feathered words are strong,
A gracious memory to buoy up and save
From Lethe's dreamless ooze, the common grave
    Of the unventurous throng.

II

Today our Reverend Mother welcomes back
  Her wisest Scholars, those who understood
The deeper teaching of her mystic tome,
  And offered their fresh lives to make it good:
    No lore of Greece or Rome,
No science peddling with the names of things,
Or reading stars to find inglorious fates,
    Can lift our life with wings
Far from Death's idle gulf that for the many waits,
    And lengthen out our dates
With that clear fame whose memory sings
In manly hearts to come, and nerves them and dilates:
Nor such thy teaching, Mother of us all!
    Not such the trumpet-call
    Of thy diviner mood,
    That could thy sons entice

From happy homes and toils, the fruitful nest
Of those half-virtues which the world calls best,
    Into war's tumult rude;
    But rather far that stern device
The sponsors chose that round thy cradle stood
    In the dim, unventured wood,
    The *Veritas* that lurks beneath
    The letter's unprolific sheath,
  Life of whate'er makes life worth living,
Seed-grain of high emprise, immortal food,
  One heavenly thing whereof earth hath the giving.

III

Many loved Truth, and lavished life's best oil
  Amid the dust of books to find her,
Content at last, for guerdon of their toil,
With the cast mantle she hath left behind her.
  Many in sad faith sought for her,
  Many with crossed hands sighed for her;
  But those, our brothers, fought for her,
  At life's dear peril wrought for her,
  So loved her that they died for her,
  Tasting the raptured fleetness
  Of her divine completeness:
  Their higher instinct knew
Those love her best who to themselves are true,
And what they dare to dream of, dare to do;
    They followed her and found her
    Where all may hope to find,
Not in the ashes of the burnt-out mind,
But beautiful with danger's sweetness round her.
    Where faith made whole with deed.
    Breathes its awakening breath
    Into the lifeless creed,
    They saw her plumed and mailed,
    With sweet, stern face unveiled,
And all-repaying eyes, look proud on them in death.

IV

Our slender life runs rippling by, and glides
  Into the silent hollow of the past;
    What is there that abides
  To make the next age better for the last?
    Is earth too poor to give us
  Something to live for here that shall outlive us?
    Some more substantial boon
Than such as flows and ebbs with Fortune's fickle moon?
    The little that we see
    From doubt is never free;
    The little that we do
    Is but half-nobly true;
    With our laborious hiving
What men call treasure, and the gods call dross,
  Life seems a jest of Fate's contriving,
  Only secure in every one's conniving,
A long account of nothings paid with loss,
Where we poor puppets, jerked by unseen wires,
  After our little hour of strut and rave,
With all our pasteboard passions and desires,
Loves, hates, ambitions, and immortal fires,
  Are tossed pell-mell together in the grave.
  But stay! no age was e'er degenerate,
  Unless men held it at too cheap a rate,
  For in our likeness still we shape our fate.
    Ah, there is something here
  Unfathomed by the cynic's sneer,
  Something that gives our feeble light
  A high immunity from night,
  Something that leaps life's narrow bars
To claim its birthright with the hosts of heaven;
  A seed of sunshine that can leaven
  Our earthly dullness with the beams of stars
      And glorify our clay

With light from fountains elder than the Day;
A conscience more divine than we,
A gladness fed with secret tears,
A vexing, forward-reaching sense
Of some more noble permanence;
A light across the sea,
Which haunts the soul and will not let it be,
Still beaconing from the heights of undegenerate years.

V

Whither leads the path
To ampler fates that leads?
Not down through flowery meads,
To reap an aftermath
Of youth's vainglorious weeds,
But up the steep, amid the wrath
And shock of deadly-hostile creeds,
Where the world's best hope and stay
By battle's flashes gropes a desperate way,
And every turf the fierce foot clings to bleeds.
Peace hath her not ignoble wreath,
Ere yet the sharp, decisive word
Light the black lips of cannon, and the sword
Dreams in its easeful sheath;
But some day the live coal behind the thought,
Whether from Baal's stone obscene,
Or from the shine serene
Of God's pure altar brought,
Bursts up in flame; the war of tongue and pen
Learns with what deadly purpose it was fraught,
And, helpless in the fiery passion caught,
Shakes all the pillared state with shock of men:
Some day the soft Ideal that we wooed
Confronts us fiercely, foe-beset, pursued,
And cries reproachful: "Was it, then, my praise,
And not myself was loved? Prove now thy truth;

I claim of thee the promise of thy youth;
Give me thy life, or cower in empty phrase,
The victim of thy genius, not its mate!"
Life may be given in many ways,
And loyalty to truth be sealed
As bravely in the closet as the field,
So bountiful is Fate;
But then to stand beside her,
When craven churls deride her,
To front a lie in arms and not to yield,
This shows, methinks, God's plan
And measure of a stalwart man,
Limbed like the old heroic breeds,
Who stands self-poised on manhood's solid earth,
Not forced to frame excuses for his birth,
Fed from within with all the strength he needs.

VI

Such was he, our Martyr-Chief,
Whom late the Nation he had led,
With ashes on her head,
Wept with the passion of an angry grief:
Forgive me, if from present things I turn
To speak what in my heart will beat and burn,
And hang my wreath on his world-honored urn.
Nature, they say, doth dote,
And cannot make a man
Save on some worn-out plan,
Repeating us by rote:
For him her Old-World moulds aside she threw,
And, choosing sweet clay from the breast
Of the unexhausted West,
With stuff untainted shaped a hero new,
Wise, steadfast in the strength of God, and true
How beautiful to see

Once more a shepherd of mankind indeed,
Who loved his charge, but never loved to lead;
One whose meek flock the people joyed to be,
Not lured by any cheat of birth,
But by his clear-grained human worth,
And brave old wisdom of sincerity!
They knew that outward grace is dust;
They could not choose but trust
In that sure-footed mind's unfaltering skill,
And supple-tempered will
That bent like perfect steel to spring again and thrust.
His was no lonely mountain-peak of mind
Thrusting to thin air o'er our cloudy bars,
A sea-mark now, now lost in vapors blind;
Broad prairie rather, genial, level-lined,
Fruitful and friendly for all human kind,
Yet also nigh to heaven and loved of loftiest stars,
Nothing of Europe here,
Or, then, of Europe fronting mornward still,
Ere any names of Serf and Peer
Could nature's equal scheme deface
And thwart her genial will;
Here was a type of the true elder race,
And one of Plutarch's men talked with us face to face.
I praise him not; it were too late;
And some innative weakness there must be
In him who condescends to victory
Such as the Present gives, and cannot wait,
Safe in himself as in a fate.
So always firmly he:
He knew to bide his time,
And can his fame abide,
Still patient in his simple faith sublime,
Till the wise years decide.
Great captains, with their guns and drums,
Disturb our judgment for the hour,

But at last silence comes;
These all are gone, and, standing like a tower,
Our children shall behold his fame,
The kindly-earnest, brave, foreseeing man,
Sagacious, patient, dreading praise, not blame,
New birth of our new soil, the first American.

VII

Long as man's hope insatiate can discern
Or only guess some more inspiring goal
Outside of Self, enduring as the pole,
Along whose course the flying axes burn
Of spirits bravely-pitched, earth's manlier brood;
Long as below we cannot find
The meed that stills the inexorable mind;
So long this faith to some ideal Good,
Under whatever mortal names it masks,
Freedom, Law, Country, this ethereal mood
That thanks the fates for their severer tasks,
Feeling its challenged pulses leap,
While others skulk in subterfuges cheap,
And, set in Danger's van, has all the boon it asks,
Shall win man's praise and woman's love,
Shall be a wisdom that we set above
All other skills and gifts to culture dear,
A virtue round whose forehead we inwreathe
Laurels that with a living passion breathe
When other crowns grow, while we twine them, sear.
What brings us thronging these high rites to pay,
And seal these hours the noblest of our year,
Save that our brothers found this better way?

VIII

We sit here in the Promised Land
That flows with Freedom's honey and milk;
But 'twas they won it, sword in hand,

Making the nettle danger soft for us as silk.
  We welcome back our bravest and our best;—
  Ah me! not all! some come not with the rest,
Who went forth brave and bright as any here!
I strive to mix some gladness with my strain,
        But the sad strings complain,
        And will not please the ear:
I sweep them for a paean, but they wane
        Again and yet again
Into a dirge, and die away, in pain.
In these brave ranks I only see the gaps,
Thinking of dear ones whom the dumb turf wraps,
Dark to the triumph which they died to gain:
    Fitlier may others greet the living,
    For me the past is unforgiving;
      I with uncovered head
      Salute the sacred dead,
Who went, and who return not.—Say not so!
'T is not the grapes of Canaan that repay,
But the high faith that failed not by the way;
Virtue treads paths that end not in the grave;
No ban of endless night exiles the brave;
        And to the saner mind
We rather seem the dead that stayed behind.
Blow, trumpets, all your exultations blow!
For never shall their aureoled presence lack;
I see them muster in a gleaming row,
With ever-youthful brows that nobler show;
We find in our dull road their shining track;
        In every nobler mood
We feel the orient of their spirit glow,
Part of our life's unalterable good,
Of all our saintlier aspiration;
        They come transfigured back,
Secure from change in their high-hearted ways,
Beautiful evermore, and with the rays
Of morn on their white Shields of Expectation!

IX

But is there hope to save
Even this ethereal essence from the grave?
What ever 'scaped Oblivion's subtle wrong
Save a few clarion names, or golden threads of song?
Before my musing eye
The mighty ones of old sweep by,
Disvoiced now and insubstantial things,
As noisy once as we; poor ghosts of kings,
Shadows of empire wholly gone to dust,
And many races, nameless long ago,
To darkness driven by that imperious gust
Of ever-rushing Time that here doth blow:
O visionary world, condition strange,
Where naught abiding is but only Change,
Where the deep-bolted stars themselves still shift and range!
Shall we to more continuance make pretence?
Renown builds tombs: a life-estate is Wit;
And, bit by bit,
The cunning years steal all from us but woe;
Leaves are we, whose decays no harvest sow.
But, when we vanish hence,
Shall they lie forceless in the dark below,
Save to make green their little length of sods,
Or deepen pansies for a year or two,
Who now to us are shining-sweet as gods?
Was dying all they had the skill to do?
That were not fruitless: but the Soul resents
Such short-lived service, as if blind events
Ruled without her, or earth could so endure;
She claims a more divine investiture
Of longer tenure than Fame's airy rents;
Whate'er she touches doth her nature share;
Her inspiration haunts the ennobled air,
Gives eyes to mountains blind,

Ears to the deaf earth, voices to the wind,
And her clear trump sings succor everywhere
By lonely bivouacs to the wakeful mind;
For soul inherits all that soul could dare:
Yea, Manhood hath a wider span
And larger privilege of life than man.
The single deed, the private sacrifice,
So radiant now through proudly-hidden tears,
Is covered up erelong from mortal eyes
With thoughtless drift of the deciduous years;
But that high privilege that makes all men peers,
That leap of heart whereby a people rise
Up to a nobler anger's height,
And, flamed on by the Fates, not shrink, but grow more bright,
That swift validity in noble veins,
Of choosing danger and disdaining shame,
Of being set on flame
By the pure fire that flies all contact base,
But wraps its chosen with angelic might,
These are imperishable gains,
Sure as the sun, medicinal as light,
These hold great futures in their lusty reins
And certify to earth a new imperial race.

X

Who now shall sneer?
Who dare again to say we trace
Our lines to a plebeian race?
Roundhead and Cavalier!
Dumb are those names erewhile in battle loud;
Dream-footed as the shadow of a cloud,
They flit across the ear:
That is best blood that hath most iron in 't.

To edge resolve with, pouring without stint
For what makes manhood dear.
Tell us not of Plantagenets,
Hapsburgs, and Guelfs, whose thin bloods crawl
Down from some victor in a border-brawl!
How poor their outworn coronets,
Matched with one leaf of that plain civic wreath
Our brave for honor's blazon shall bequeath,
Through whose desert a rescued Nation sets
Her heel on treason, and the trumpet hears
Shout victory, tingling Europe's sullen ears
With vain resentments and more vain regrets!

XI

Not in anger, not in pride,
Pure from passion's mixture rude
Ever to base earth allied,
But with far-heard gratitude,
Still with heart and voice renewed,
To heroes living and dear martyrs dead,
The strain should close that consecrates our brave.
Lift the heart and lift the head!
Lofty be its mood and grave,
Not without a martial ring,
Not without a prouder tread
And a peal of exultation:
Little right has he to sing
Through whose heart in such an hour
Beats no march of conscious power,
Sweeps no tumult of elation!
'T is no Man we celebrate,
By his country's victories great,
A hero half, and half the whim of Fate,
But the pith and marrow of a Nation
Drawing force from all her men,
Highest, humblest, weakest, all,

For her time of need, and then
Pulsing it again through them,
Till the basest can no longer cower,
Feeling his soul spring up divinely tall,
Touched but in passing by her mantle-hem.
Come back, then, noble pride, for 't is her dower!
How could poet ever tower,
If his passions, hopes, and fears,
If his triumphs and his tears,
Kept not measure with his people?
Boom, cannon, boom to all the winds and waves!
Clash out, glad bells, from every rocking steeple!
Banners, advance with triumph, bend your staves!
And from every mountain-peak,
Let beacon-fire to answering beacon speak,
Katahdin tell Monadnock, Whiteface he,
And so leap on in light from sea to sea,
Till the glad news be sent
Across a kindling continent,
Making earth feel more firm and air breathe braver:
"Be proud! for she is saved, and all have helped to save her!
She that lifts up the manhood of the poor,
She of the open soul and open door,
With room about her hearth for all mankind!
The fire is dreadful in her eyes no more;
From her bold front the helm she doth unbind,
Sends all her handmaid armies back to spin,
And bids her navies, that so lately hurled
Their crashing battle, hold their thunders in,
Swimming like birds of calm along the unharmful shore.
No challenge sends she to the elder world,
That looked askance and hated; a light scorn
Plays o'er her mouth, as round her mighty knees
She calls her children back, and waits the morn
Of nobler day, enthroned between her subject seas."

XII

Bow down, dear Land, for thou hast found release!
  Thy God, in these distempered days,
  Hath taught thee the sure wisdom of His ways,
And through thine enemies hath wrought thy peace!
  Bow down in prayer and praise!
No poorest in thy borders but may now
Lift to the juster skies a man's enfranchised brow.
O Beautiful! my Country! ours once more!
Smoothing thy gold of war-dishevelled hair
O'er such sweet brows as never other wore,
  And letting thy set lips,
  Freed from wrath's pale eclipse,
The rosy edges of their smile lay bare,
What words divine of lover or of poet
Could tell our love and make thee know it,
Among the Nations bright beyond compare?
  What were our lives without thee?
  What all our lives to save thee?
  We reck not what we gave thee;
  We will not dare to doubt thee,
But ask whatever else, and we will dare!

James Russell Lowell
(*Massachusetts*)

INDEX OF TITLES

Index of Titles

Index of Titles

Index of Titles

INDEX OF AUTHORS

Index of Authors

Index of Authors